MASTERCLASS COLOURING

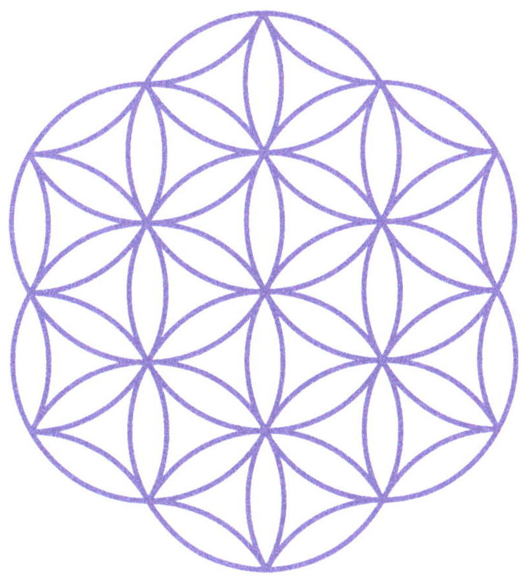

FOREST DREAMING

Written and Illustrated by
Greg C Grace

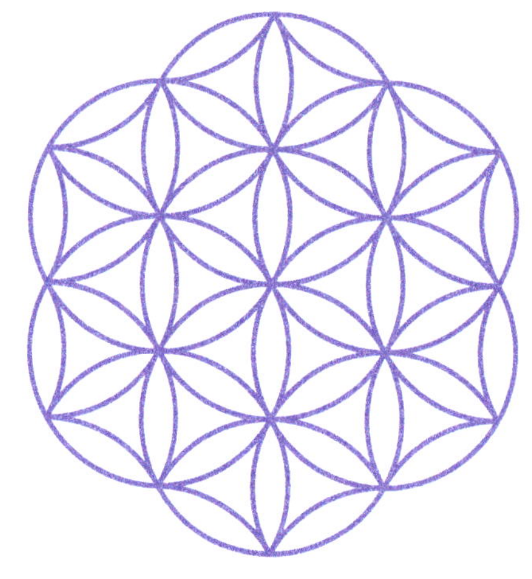

MASTERCLASS COLOURING

FOREST DREAMING

Written and Illustrated

by

Greg C Grace

ISBN: 9780994461940

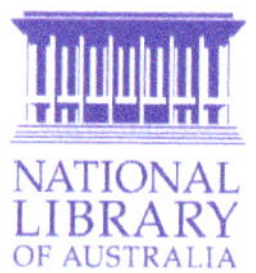

A catalogue record for this work is available from the National Library of Australia

CONTENTS

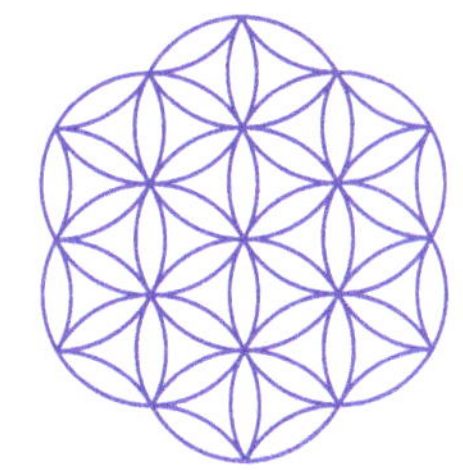

About the Author

Greg C Grace is an innovative and visionary artist who lives in Adelaide, South Australia. Imersed for over 20 years within the wider artistic community, helping define the boundaries of where consciousness and creativity meet.

Adept in the fields of Sacred Geometry, Mandalas, Comparative Cosmology, and Dreamtime Art, he is also a renowned Vedic Astrologer and Personal Vastu Consultant, studying deeply and practicing in these arts since 2001. His published works include over a dozen titles, including domains such as: Colouring; Drawing; Graphic Symbolism; Gems & Crystals – along with the creation of several innovative 'How to draw' and interractive 'Graphic Design' Series.

Greg has a wealth of experience in the fields of Jyotish, Ayurveda, Transpersonal Therapy, Chromotherapy and Orthomolecular Nutrition. He is an accomplished Environmental & Wildlife Photographer, specialising in the domains of Gems and Minerals, Location Photography, Environmental and Species Impact, Native Birds, Flora and Fauna. His vivid and impactful images have been utilised the world over in such publications as 'The New York Post' and 'BBC Wildlife Magazine'. He has amassed one of the world's largest specialty stock libraries through countless photographic sessions over the years and on his travels in Australia and trips abroad.

With his inspirational techniques and vast store of creative wisdom, Greg has seen great success practicing as a Project, Branding and Personal Development Consultant for over 15 years. His clients include various Organisations, Individuals, Business Developers and Entrepreneurs. His accumulated wisdom and boundless appreciation for all mediums of creativity have made him a sought out figure in the realms of Written and Visual Storytelling, Art Direction, Project Development, Artistic Symbolism and Cross-cultural Cosmology.

Greg's comprehensive work as a Designer, Art Director and Project Developer has led to a broader and more user-friendly approach towards teaching, mentoring and the very conception of this 'Masterclass Series'. He hopes to continue his life journey of sharing creative inspiration and empowering wisdom for many years to come.

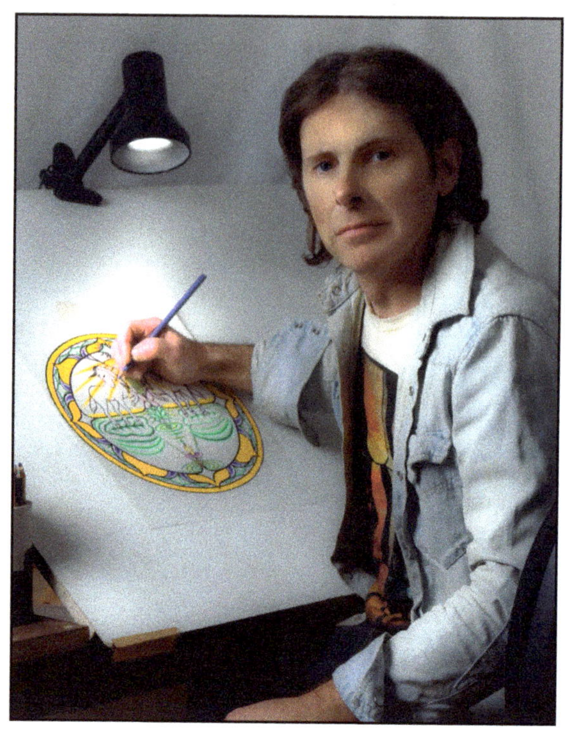

Follow Greg C Grace:

www.gregcgracephotography.com or visit him @gregcgrace on Instagram, or on linkedin to access websites, stock libraries, portfolios, published works/titles, work history, current & future colouring projects.

~ This Book is dedicated to '***OUR***' Mother, '***Mother Earth***', who has brought many awesome and diverse experiences my way over the years through the world of nature. I feel truely grateful for the many precious moments and valuable resources made available from this Earth journey and it is my aim to share this gratitude with the people of Earth through my work as a photographer, Artist and illustrator. For our Earth journey 'captured through time' tells a invaluable tale that visual storytelling aims to imortalise and portray. So this one goes out with love and Appreciation to 'Earth' and all her forest creatures grand or small and to all those who warrant or seek to preserve her precious natural Ecosystems and self-maintained resources and terrains we call home.

Introduction

Journey deep into the world of woodland creatures, with this latest Masterclass Colouring instalment that ventures deep into the 'Forests of Earth'. The forest is alive with and endless array of species that convey the essential diversity of manifest creation. It represents the very fertile ground or growth potential of our creative aspirations. Graphic styles in this volume depict: Scenic, Aerial, Mandala and Window-style art panels, that explore diverse forest lands and enchanted woodland worlds. Explore enigmatic forest creatures and exotic scenic lands, along with a variety of birds, fruits, flowers and native trees to further enliven your colouring experience. This '12 Masterclass' volume is abundant with insightful numerical and colour symbolism, along with dedicated colour-wheel tuition.

Throughout my life, I have been lucky enough to take many country and overseas trips to spend time out in nature. Growing up, our family lived surrounded by parks and creeks and we spent time on the holidays in many outback and coastal locations. My dad kept birds in large walkthrough aviaries - with exotic parrots, finches, doves and quails from around the world. This secured my love for birds when I was out in nature and later when I went on to become a nature and wildlife photographer. Australia has some beautiful country and forest locations indeed, from the more sparse and rocky woodland plains of South Australia, to the thick dense rainforests of Queensland's 'Daintree'. Wildlife from one region to the next is diverse and awe-inspiring for both a nature enthusiast and a documentary wildlife photographer.

Visiting some rare and unique wildlife sanctuaries such as the Hawaiian rainforests, and remote island forests of South Thailand have been a great source of inspiration for me over the years. In this volume I have tried to include animals from the continents of Australia, Africa, North and South America, along with rare and endangered animals like our beloved tiger species and rare birds and exotic island species. On my photographic journeys I encounter the very energetic signature of these scenic lands and aim to encapsulate these in my artwork and the very progression of the greater Masterclass Colouring Art Series. This volume has a wider variety or flower and tree species, along with their folklore and esoteric meaning to help further complement your colouring experience, making for a more multidimensional journey.

The 'Forest Dreaming' Volume sets the stage for a rich array of bird life that make for great colouring subjects. Songbirds, parrots, wrens and swallows feature strongly, along with the swift and hummingbird, which share the same bird family (Order of Adopiformes). Some of the birds may be portrayed as a generic songbird, finch or parrot, while the Madagascan kingfisher or macaw are more regionally specific. To complement the birds a great deal of flowers and forest trees help visually support your colouring journey. These each have their own symbolic syntax which is further explored, along with shared colouring insights relative to their deeper meaning.

Animals totems are unique and fascinating, from the most basic symbolism understood by a child, to the more diverse and transpersonal meanings and application. They have great value in the world of art and symbolism. On my journey as an artist, totems are found not only to be a useful tool for graphic art depiction and enriched stylisation, yet seem to hold an inter-connective capacity between species, a kind of universal language of life. Life is full of contrast and polarity, from the gentle beauty of the butterfly to the rich and deep legends and folklore of the bat. In the bird kingdom we have the subtle, yet stunning colour display and iridescense of the hummingbird, to the more majestic power of the eagle. A wide scope of creatures and lifeforms from the animal, vegetable and mineral kingdoms appear to help ground the totemic aspect of our journey, which at times is as simple as parrots nestled in a grove of cherry blossoms.

It is my vision that in sharing my insights and bringing together wisdom from the worlds of 'forest' and 'colour', that you may discover an ever-expansive sense of mystery and wonder through the greater exploration of creativity and colour.

Overview of the Series

The Masterclass Colouring Series is an exciting and innovative progressive Art Series, with the latest theme for this instalment being the 'Forests of the World'. Each book in the series is based around a signature hue, with this volume's being 'green'. Defined in this instalment as the vivid and bright green of new growth and renewal. The hue range of green ranges from the invigorating warm lime green, through balancing and neutralising grass or leaf greens, to the slightly cool and calming hues of emerald or aqua green. Then there are slightly turbid or tawny greens, along with slightly pastel versions like apple, mint or seafoam green. Green is a hue range which we all identify with through the green of nature and the plant kingdom. Associated with creative renewal, it promotes growth in our aspirational endeavours. It is favoured among earth-loving creative types for its ability to help keep us 'fertile' in our creatively capacity. It is a hue range that helps activate creative thought and further enliven our creative capacity or endeavours.

Green can be a gently passive or sattvic (neither dulling or exciting) hue in its softer pastel emerald and aqua hues, yet green in general is more rajasic (activating). It represents slightly active qualities closer to the yellow hues, which are also considered sattvic, providing they are not too bright, in which they become warming or heating in excess. These hues are however not as directly activating or rajasic as the red hue range. In the pages ahead suggestions are given for ways to complement or work with 'green' as the signature theme hue for this volume. Aim for utilising the full gamut of green's potential to help activate and enliven, as the forest theme really makes for fertile ground and some secure potential for the activation of creativity and self renewal on our colouring journey.

In this volume, there are more Numerological and Astrological references given, along with key numbers and symbolism that is woven into the fabric of many of the dreamtime stories and panel designs. As this volume is dedicated to the 'Earth' element and the magical world of the forest, majestic totems like forest cats, or the ancient and wonderous 'kangaroo' appear to highlight Earth's awe-inspiring diversity of species. Masterclasses further highlight the characteristics of individual species like forest birds, or the variety and exotic appeal of certain forest flowers or blooms. Panels suggest ways to work with various hues of the green range as a backdrop or background canvas, like we find in the green of nature. In this regard, some panels may benefit from thinking of how to utilise and place green at the very beginning. Other applications envision just how to make the panel 'sing', give impact, or become further 'alive'.

As we move deeper into the exploration of colour and the full gamut of green, you may choose to think directly of the complementary effects to green of certain hues like violet, magenta, or the 'direct opposite' red. Red can be be used in a variety of ways with a variety of green hues for interesting and contrasting effects. For example, as the red hue moves towards orange, we can shift the companion green hue towards aqua. Alternatively, pastel reds give rise to soft pale 'pinks', which bring great contrast with either deep cool greens or soft apple and pastel mint greens. Even burgundy, which is like a deep red or deep magenta can complement very well with apple green and pastel aqua or emerald green hues. Violet also complements a whole host of green hues and brings a certain magic which we see in the world of exotic rainforest flowers and orchid blooms. Green can be seen as the very fabric of Creation, depicting the deeper exploration of the woodland and forest realms.

A lot of thought goes into the conception of content for the Masterclass Colouring Series - some 300-plus hours per volume for the concept drawings, ink renderings and colouring examples alone. Not to mention crafting the masterclass text entries and series cover designs. It is important to mention that all line artwork is produced freehand, even circles and straight lines. The odd circle tracing device or coin may have been used on base pencil to give symmetry, yet the overlying ink art is always drawn freehand. On the colouring side, panels and exercises contained within have a balance of hand and digital colouring, with more hand-coloured examples intended to appear as the series progresses. Digital colouring often transfers better to printing and displays more consistent colour hues that otherwise don't hold up to the scrutiny of the print process. Also, people will choose either to use colour pencils or ink pens. This is an individual's personal choice that I respect and I do not wish to preach to any particular medium, niche or colour genre. Also, there are options such as watercolour pens, metallics or neons.

Some exercises such as we see in Masterclass #2 include duplicate designs that were coloured in various hues, to show distinctly how to create specific colour combinations that achieve a desired effect. Some designs have a degree of hand colouring with accents or outer panel backgrounds coloured in the digital arena. However, this volume utilises predominantly the CMYK colour space in a way to get the most vivid and captivating array of colours. Further exploringthe subtle nuances of colour balance, it expands our awareness of colour knowledge.

With the Masterclass Series panels, a great deal more time is spent inking. Getting the correct line density that is ideal for both ink and colour pencils is essential. For example, drawing and inking a standard colouring page with simple line pens takes around 3 to 4 hours, with the panels in this book most often taking 8-10 hours each. Some degree of inconsistency between line work in the panels may still exist, as some panels had to be enlarged or condensed to fit the A4 format. To compensate, some panels are included as a dual-page spread instead of the single page format. In designing the panels for inclusion in each volume, some artwork may appear from previous titles. This is usually less than ten percent and warrants inclusion along subject specific lines. Another example would be a panel that was coloured in a previous book, yet not given full colour decryption or breakdown in that volume, in terms of colour distribution or colour symmetry. The colour guides in the final two masterclasses are also designed for multi-use application through the emerging Masterclass Series.

Colouring in with pencils often calls for a different approach than with ink pens. Ink pens often give a bolder, more vivid or colour-saturated effect. Pencils are easier to blend and shade with, allowing for different layers of colour density or colour tones to be mixed together, built up or applied. Ink pens however are less forgiving in colour shading and blending applications. Bright or bold colours can also be applied more softly with pencils to get pastel effects from what would be an otherwise fully-saturated or vivid hue. Some artists even use both inks and pencils in the same panel to achieve more contrasting or striking effects. This can work especially well with accent colours in ink that might otherwise be unachievable from pencils alone - like neons, metallics, silver or gold. So, in terms of application, I try not to get too caught up in the wide array of materials and mediums available to today's colourist. At times it may be preferable to test various combinations of ink pens together with soft and hard pencils on photocopied versions, which is allowed for private study under the copyright act. This can help rule out potential incompatible colour choices, colour density issues between the various mediums, or uncover discordant colour notes or combinations that just don't sit right together. Alternatively, it can identify conflictual or contrasting opposites, if this is what you are going for or what elements or areas of an image calls for.

When colouring smaller and ornate designs with ink pens, you generally get a certain amount of bleed from the ink absorbing into the paper. With pencils however, you tend to apply more pressure and colour somewhat faster than you do with ink pens. Alternatively, some people choose to colour in a soft pastel style with pencils, to channel a subtler, more ethereal feel into their artwork. Another point is the need for a spine on printed products, which encroaches into the middle of the artwork on some panels. It is often helpful to cut some pages out with a cutting knife and colour on a hard surface for pencils to get better colour saturation. In many panels the line density is designed slightly thicker to allow for a more pleasant colouring experience – for the last thing we want to add to our relaxing pastime is the frustration of not being able to colour cleanly between line segments. Also, not all of us have the same degree of youthful vigour in our eyesight, which is also factored into the panel and overall series design. The future aim is to provide a website that will give options for larger panels, as some of the panels are better suited to a larger A3 format. There will even be larger canvas options where designs can be painted for use as decoration or environmental enhancement in the home.

**Watch for direct weblinks appearing on my Instagram and LinkedIn page and for these exciting new products and theme-based colouring kits in the year ahead. As a website and larger colouring kits become available, there will be many options for larger sizes and even 'faint outline' canvases suitable for acrylic and oil painting.*

Masterclass 1: Creating and Understanding Colour Wheels.

Many theories and models exist on how to utilise the colour wheel. Some present a more generalised or superficial understanding of colour, while others may represent a colour model from a self-limiting perspective or personal bias, without explaining the core qualities or practical value of individual colours. Study the colour wheels below and supporting volume text and come to your own conclusions as to how you can best utilise colour in your artwork and personal colouring experience. No one model is inherently right or wrong, with the colour wheels in the Masterclass Series even being refined for each volume. To avoid getting bogged down in lofty colour theory, let's look at some fundamental basics of the colour wheel geared towards practical application. Also, see the colour qualities section in 'Masterclass 12' for further valuable insights and for deeper experimentation on your colouring journey.

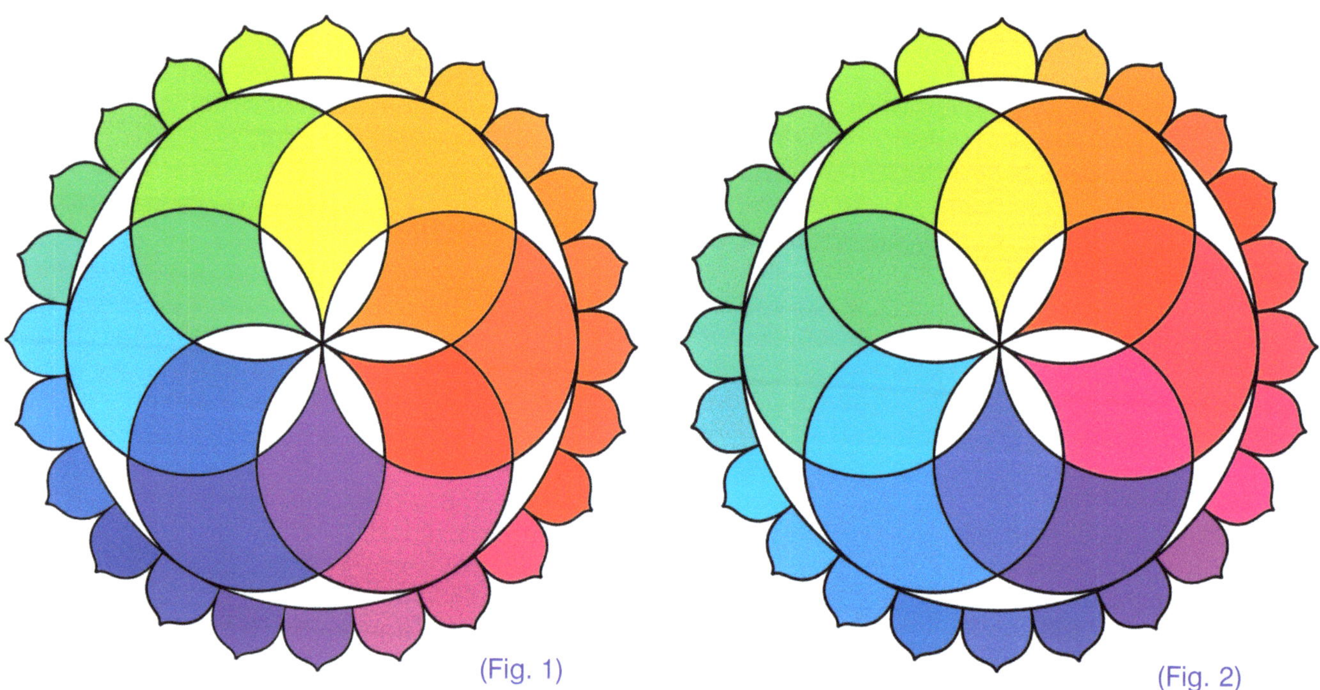

(Fig. 1) (Fig. 2)

Colour wheel (Fig. 1) is constructed from six base complementary opposite colours and forms the basis of many colour models. It works through how colours impact the psyche and mind, and to how human vision interracts with colours in the natural world. The complementary opposite of 'hot-red' for example is 'cool green', like we see in traffic lights. Staring at a hot-red triangle on a white card for some time, then immediately looking to a blank white card, we will see a colour-opposite green version of the same image for a short period. This is due to a sympathetic resonance and equilibrium being attained in relation to the principles of how we process colour through the eyes at a core level.

The centre six petals of the colour wheel (Fig. 2) are constructed from two sets of primary colours: (1) 'Subtractive Primaries' (Cyan, Yellow and Magenta) used for inks, pigments and paints in the art and print trade; (2) 'Additive Primaries' (Red, Green and Blue) for digital colour monitors, photography and admixtures of coloured or additive light. If we put the two together to form the base six hues of the (Fig. 2) colour wheel, they work fine for the utilisation of distinct colour hues up to the twelve-point colour wheel. However, as we expand beyond the twelve in equal measure, and progress to a 24-point colour wheel, there starts to become neighbouring colours which are a bit too similar and not distinct steps from one hue to another. This is most evident in an over-abundance of the red and green colour hues, at the expense of, or minimal representation of, the gold-orange and violet/purple hues.

Likewise, with (Fig. 1) - as we expand into the 24 petal hues, we see the opposite to (Fig.2), with an over-abundance here in the orange hue zones, with a lesser representation of the aqua and red zones. Neither offer an ideal or balanced colour wheel for practical application. For this reason the 21-point colour wheel (Fig. 3) was developed with more integrative and step-progressive colouring in mind.

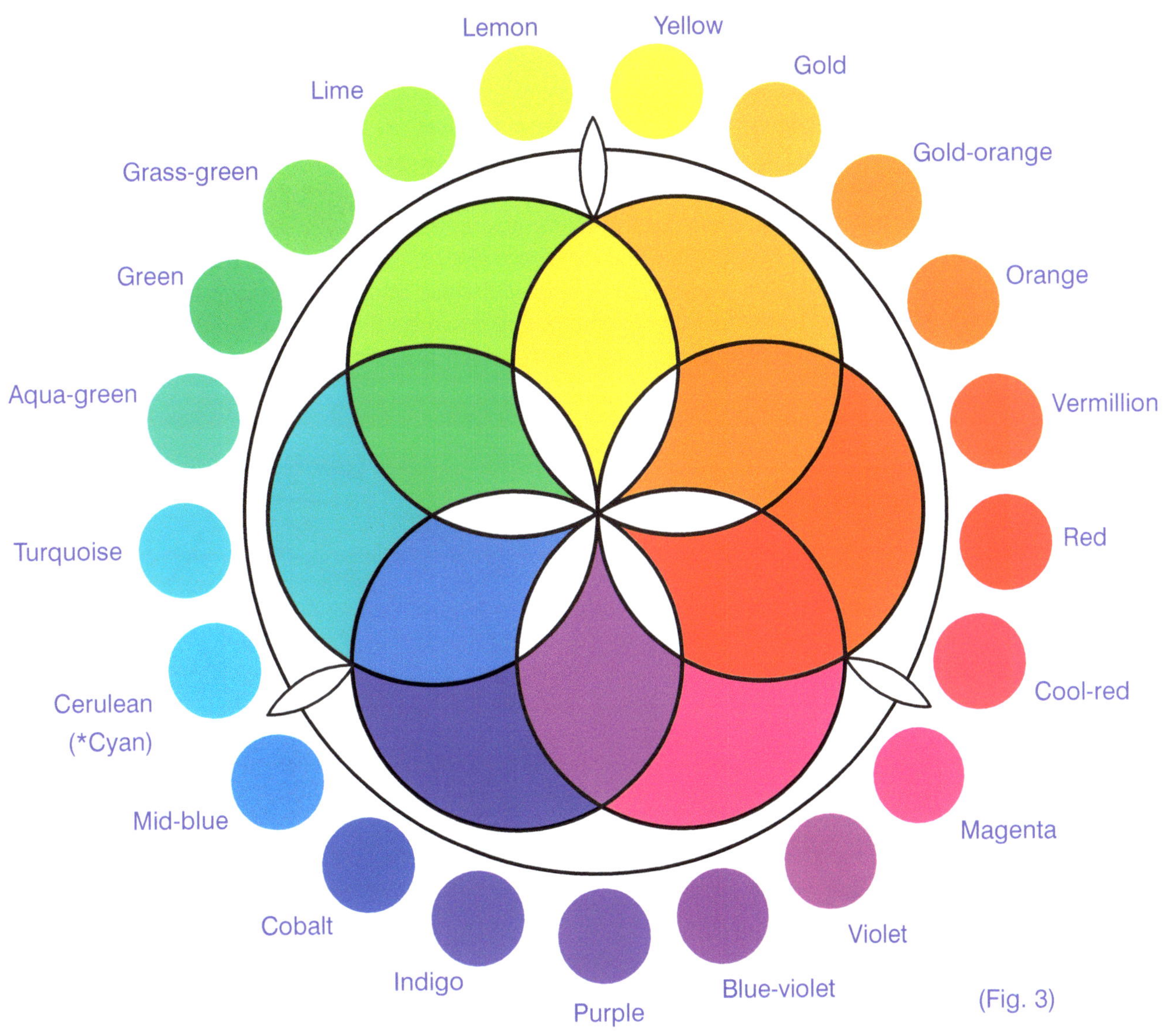

(Fig. 3)

It is easy to introduce limitations at the very core level of colour wheel construction. We risk creating a 'less than ideal' colour progression at the outer and most-usable expansion of the colour wheel. We may also produce a colour wheel unsuitable for colouring effectively and creating our most impactful artworks. If colours chosen to be used next to each other in artwork are too similar, the image can lose visual impact or vibrancy. With these points in mind, the ideal for practical colour definition seems to be a '21-point' colour wheel, in terms of a distinct colour phase progression. Beyond this the human eye starts to lose its sense of defined boundaries in terms of what might be considered a distinct step in hue progression. These 21 hue values (Fig.3) are named for convenience sake and in support of the practical step progressional model. However, it is important to not get too caught up in the names, as we each have a different understanding of colour on account of our mental conditioning and learnt association between colour as a subject and our experiences in the outer world.

So study the various colour wheels and dive deep into the medium of colour to create you art pieces. Be prepared to doubt and question what you once thought to be a set boundary in your knowledge and application of colour. In studying colour theory and colour models a bit of confusion is a good thing, as it fosters a deeper inquiry into the multifaceted potential of the many diverse and wonderful hues on offer. Any one hue is merely a snapshot or partial solidification of light rays, either suspended in matter by the application of a paint or pigment, or given off and accentuated as reflected light. We are just lucky on our colouring journey that we can define boundaries and bold representations of colour through the use of inks, pencils and paints. Alternatively, we may seek a more fluid or open expression of the subtle nuances of colour in its capacity to provide variations of lighter, less-saturated or softer pastel hues.

*(*Cyan is the ink hue close to Cerulean or Sky-blue)*

Masterclass 2: Colours Contemplation for the Squirrel Panel.

Complementary colours can be utilised in a number of ways in our artwork and graphic designs. In this exercise we will focus on colours that signify the vibrant and invigorating energies of 'Spring'. I thought to remove the window style black ink framework of the image and just concentrate on the integral colours that bring life to the image and storyline depiction. This way we get to see first hand just how the colours intermingle in what is otherwise a design with more fixed boundaries, or segemted colour domains. What this shares is a more open and free-flowing colour dynamic. We also see precisely how variations of pastels sit nicely against the more solid or vivid colour hues like the cyan, electric blue and bold bright greens. Finally, the caramel, chocolate and slightly rustic brown hues bring earthiness and cohesiveness to the design. For a further in-depth look at the colour syntax and full colour breakdown on this design, see Masterclass 4 on Page 14. Also, to explore more on the colour palette swatches, look ahead to Masterclass 11 on Page 80.

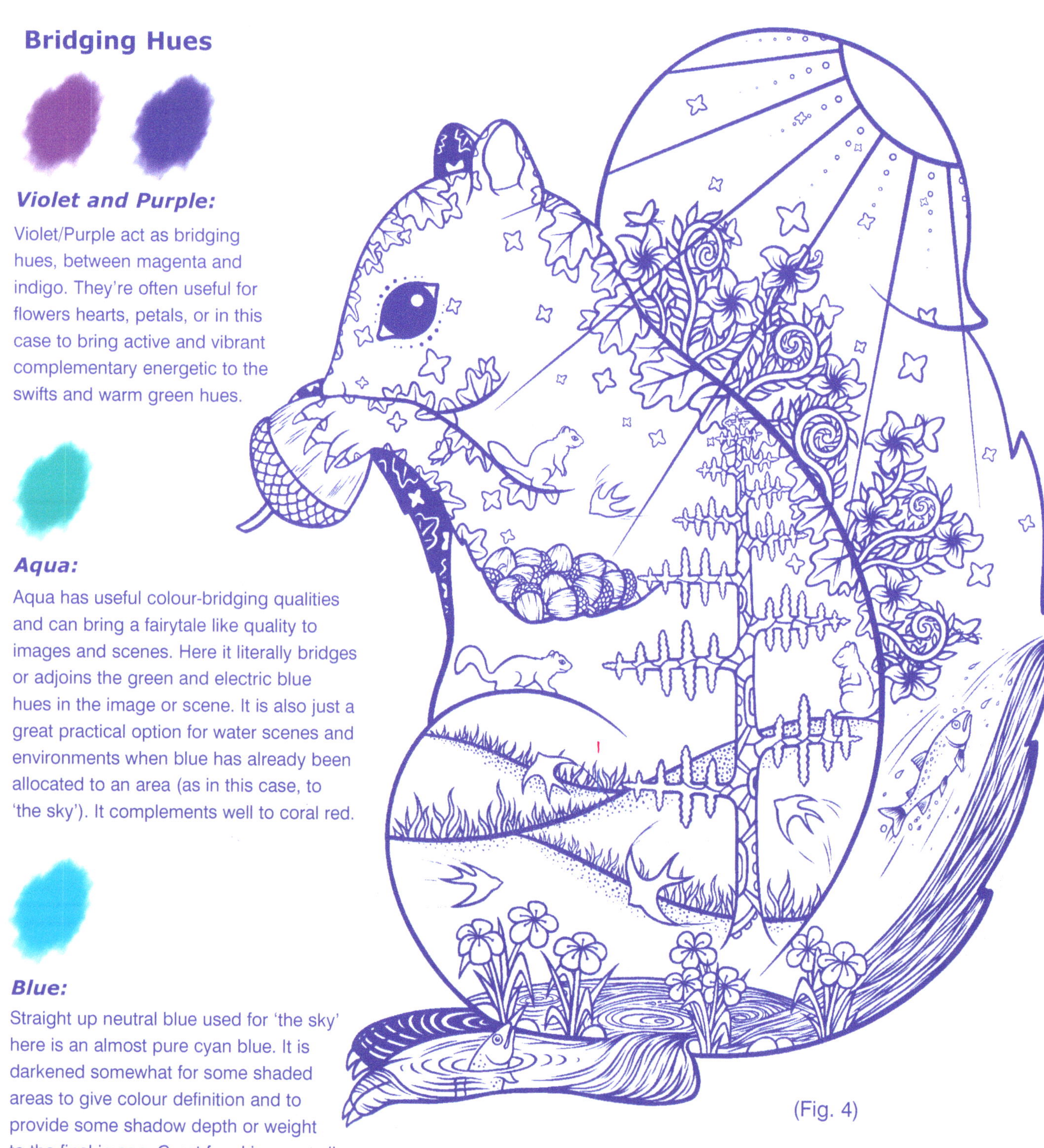

Bridging Hues

Violet and Purple:

Violet/Purple act as bridging hues, between magenta and indigo. They're often useful for flowers hearts, petals, or in this case to bring active and vibrant complementary energetic to the swifts and warm green hues.

Aqua:

Aqua has useful colour-bridging qualities and can bring a fairytale like quality to images and scenes. Here it literally bridges or adjoins the green and electric blue hues in the image or scene. It is also just a great practical option for water scenes and environments when blue has already been allocated to an area (as in this case, to 'the sky'). It complements well to coral red.

Blue:

Straight up neutral blue used for 'the sky' here is an almost pure cyan blue. It is darkened somewhat for some shaded areas to give colour definition and to provide some shadow depth or weight to the final image. Great for skies over all.

(Fig. 4)

Invigorating Hues

Hues like bold vibrant yellow and warm pastel pink are excellent to wake up an image and are great for sunrises and the invigorating energies of Spring. This pink hue is softened somewhat in what is termed 'hot pink'- actually close to solid magenta on the colour wheel.

Accent Hues

Coral red and light grey and are pivotal in that they provide colour contrast and colour relief, especially in the aqua-hued watery environment towards the base of the image.

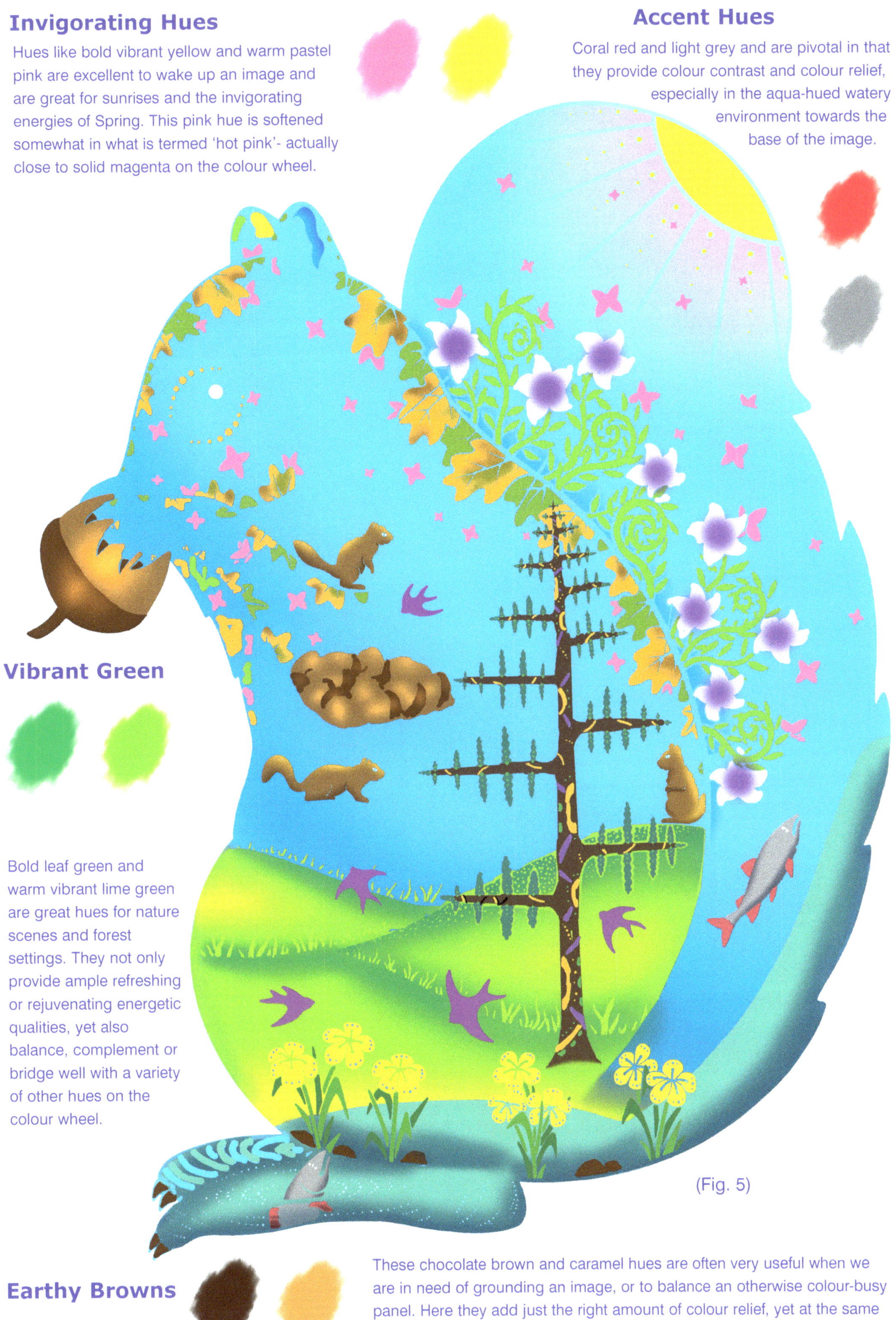

Vibrant Green

Bold leaf green and warm vibrant lime green are great hues for nature scenes and forest settings. They not only provide ample refreshing or rejuvenating energetic qualities, yet also balance, complement or bridge well with a variety of other hues on the colour wheel.

(Fig. 5)

Earthy Browns

These chocolate brown and caramel hues are often very useful when we are in need of grounding an image, or to balance an otherwise colour-busy panel. Here they add just the right amount of colour relief, yet at the same time work well with the vivacious energies of the 'Squirrel' totem.

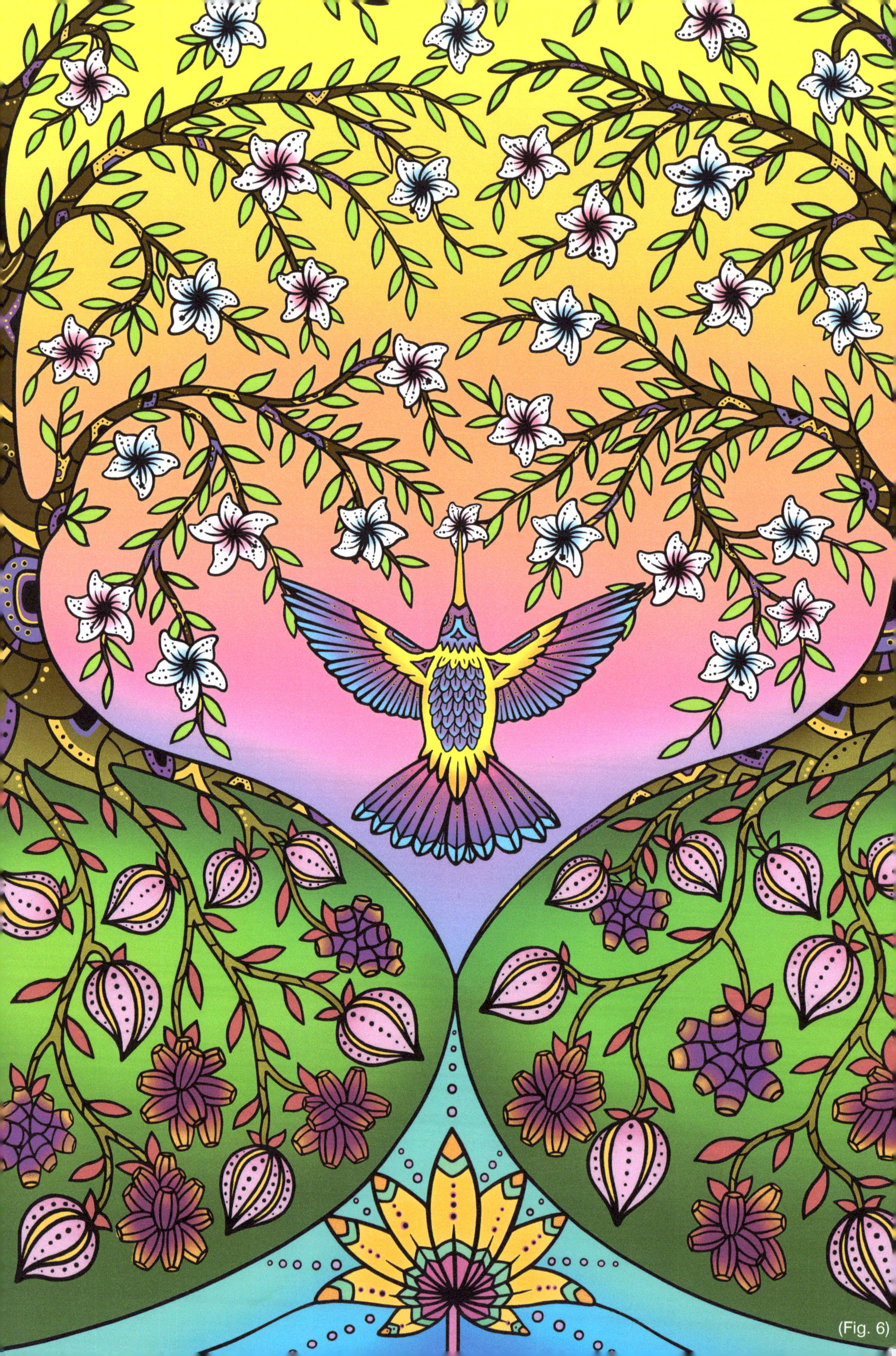

(Fig. 6)

Masterclass 3: Colour Choices for the Forest Hummingbird.

Shading Techniques:

Shading in this panel is mainly evident in the subtle variations of the morning sky, where a nice balance of colours bring a sense of transformation from one daylight stage to another. Further colour shading of interest and that gives great impact is the shading on the hummingbirds wings, which really lifts the image and brings the panel alive with colour vibrancy. Lastly, the flower center hues are shaded with some white left around the outer edge. This gives a feeling of lightness and brings necessary colour relief to the overall artwork's play of colour.

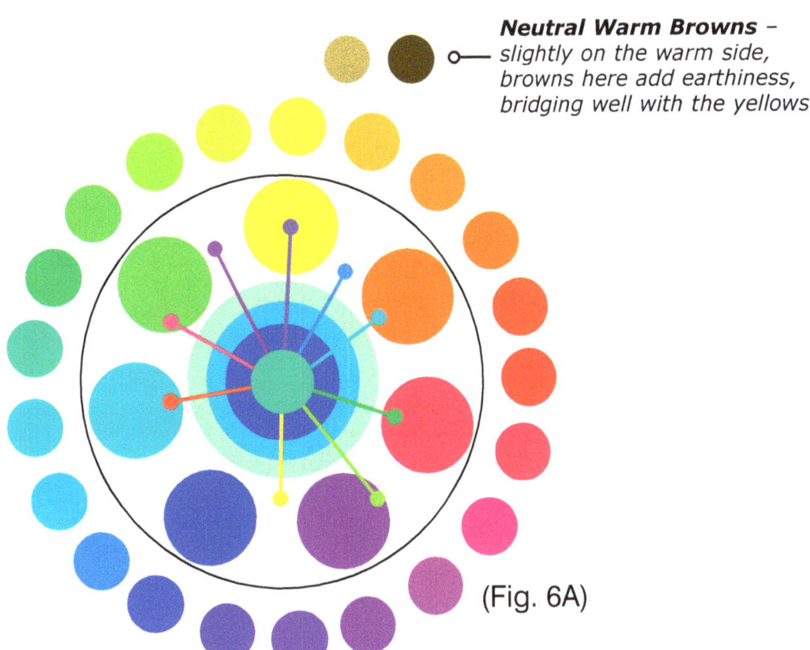

(Fig. 6A)

Colour distribution:

The overall balance of this panel is achieved in a number of ways. The predominant colours to emphasise the principles of joy and expansion associated with the hummingbird totem are encapsulated within the yellow and violet hue admixture. Elements of subtle and bold contrast add impact through the shading of violet, electric blue or turquoise hues on the hummingbird wing tips. Whatever colours you choose, try and keep the hummingbird colours vibrant and alive, as it should look like it is in motion or feel activating to some degree. Then there is a good degree of balance provided between the complementary opposites of the burgundy, oranges, pink and green tones on the bottom half of the image. If you look to the colour distribution wheel, you will see nice groupings of colours, by where a colour chosen for an area is widened somewhat to include two to three hues from a colour range.

(Fig. 6B)

Forest Hummingbird - (Fig. 6) - The first vision I had with this image was to see the trees rich with chocolate brown and caramel hues, contrasted with a nice expansive light-yellow. Then I had a general idea to mix in the chosen hummingbird colours on the tree accents, to make the forest come alive and bring further invigoration into the image. The hummingbird totem relates to joy and transformation, with colours suiting these traits woven into the panel design. The design is very expansive and full of colour symmetry that relates to expansion and the principle of abundance. Two aspects of the Wisdom Goddess have been fashioned in also, with the colours for the top half conveying expasion into sacred space. The clorours and symbolism of the bottom half relate to the auspicious energies of the Goddess of abundance and wealth. Together it is a very vibrant and expansive colouring experience. You may choose colours suggested here or feel inclinded to add your own chnages, or even colour the whole thing in a completely different style altogether.

Where this image works well is with its balance of complementary colours. The bottom half of the image I went for earthy and fertile colours, that you would see in the invigorating foliage of nature and the ripeness of fruits and berries. Then to add further colour dynamics, the lotus was coloured in bold and contrasting hues along with the water section. Colours were carefully chosen here to keep a certain colour relief and to further complement hues from the top half of the image. The sky was chosen to have a clear twlight effect, yet also to emphasise the yellow and golden hues in the shaded gradient of colour. This way the image clearly gets lighter and more expansive towards the top and suggests lighting from a subdued or somewhat distant source. This brings dimension and depth to the image. Try and think in this regard when planning your own sky colours and any subtle accents you may choose. Lastly, I decided to add two complementary colours for the flower centres of pink-violet and aqua. These particular colours finished off the sky's contrast nicely and brought a lighthearted feel.

Masterclass 4: Examining Colours for the Squirrel Panel.

Shading Techniques:

Colour shading with this panel is more subtle and mainly applied to give volume and depth to the image. Sky sections always benefit from shading to accentuate the radiant light of the sun, especially with panels like this which call for bold illumination. Shading on the acorns and squirrels is just to emphasise their placement relative to the sun, which provides the source of light for most shaded image elements, except the flowers and autumn leaves. With the flowers, radial shading emphasising the soft purple hue was the final accentuation of colour. Witht he autumn leaves, three-hue variegation gave a nice earthy balance and bridged well with other objects and elements in the image.

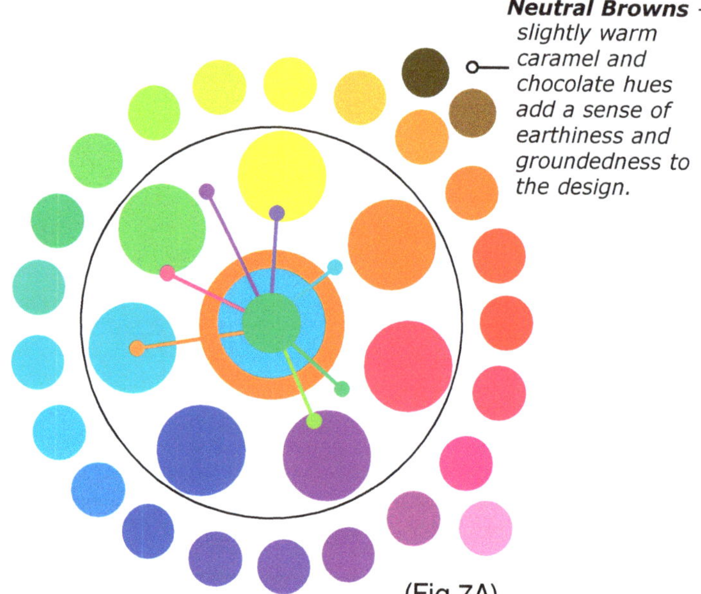

(Fig.7A)

Colour distribution:

Colour distribution here is decidedly less busy and more spatially applied. Background colours are divided into the 3 main domains of 'Earth' (Green), 'Sky' (Blue) and 'Water' (Aqua). We then see the golden and saffron-hued highlights well placed throughout the image, which gives the image 'liveliness' and further emphasising visual impact. Likewise, the violet-pink butterflies provide gently-active colour relief and bring a certain lightness or life of their own. Lastly, the deep violet and purplish hues provide further balance as, like neutral green (between cool-green and warm lime green), this purple hue range is right in the middle of cool blue and warm violet, bringing about an appeasing, equalising or balancing effect. There is a clear sense of earthiness and balance in the overall colour distribution, yet at the same time the colour signature is uplifting and clearly in the vibrant realm of 'Spring'.

(Fig. 7B)

Squirrel Panel (Fig.7) - This panel was conceived to depict the vibrant and fertile energies of 'Spring'. The 'Squirrel' totem is a very active and vivacious one. Matched with the 'Butterfly', 'Swift' and 'Salmon' totems, we have an interesting syntax or storyline indeed. All 4 totems relate to fertility and abundance in one capacity or another. Colours chosen here were a mix of nature-identical and totemic qualities, with characteristic traits embodied being further accentuated by wise colour choice. There is a nice balance in the overall composure and less-complex placement of hues. The sky blue hues are generally devoid of any yellow, which contrasts well with the saffron and amber golds. Likewise, the fertile warm green hues mimic the vibrant renewal of spring growth. These are accented by the shaded 'deeper cool or neutral green' section, which bring the image down to earth and makes for an even more complementary match with the violet swift figures.

Colours for the swifts were chosen here to provide balance, as they relate to the hot pink, violet, through to mid purple hue range. Providing bold contrast here with their complementary opposite hues of lime green and warm greens, they symbolise abundance manifesting, coming out of the ether (void) and into the air realm. You will also see the yellow spring flowers complementing well the mid-purple-violet swifts, bringing in even more abundance, expansion and new potential for growth. The salmon are coloured to provide a pivotal accent environment, with the contrasting emerald or aqua water hues, neutral or cool silver-grey, with the bold coral-red fins. The hue for the butterflies was carefully chosen until just the right balance of pink and soft violet was achieved, not too deep and not too light. Likewise, the hibiscus style blooms were chosen to match the swift colours, which gave the panel its final momentum, spiralling in manifestation and potential for greater growth. The warm caramel and cinnamon hues were chosen to add earthiness and signify here the actual manifestation of abundance and potential growth in the physicality of the material world.

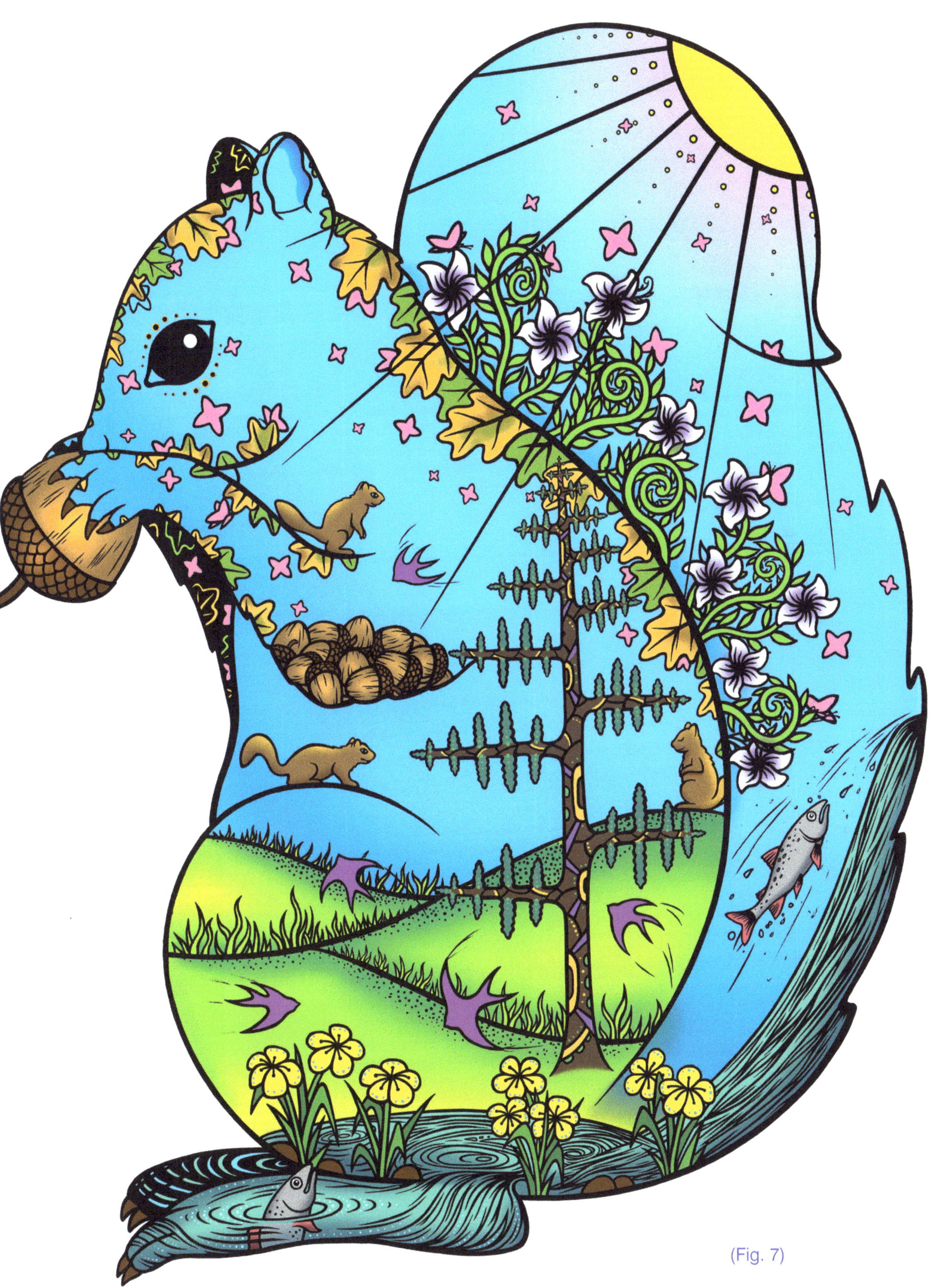

(Fig. 7)

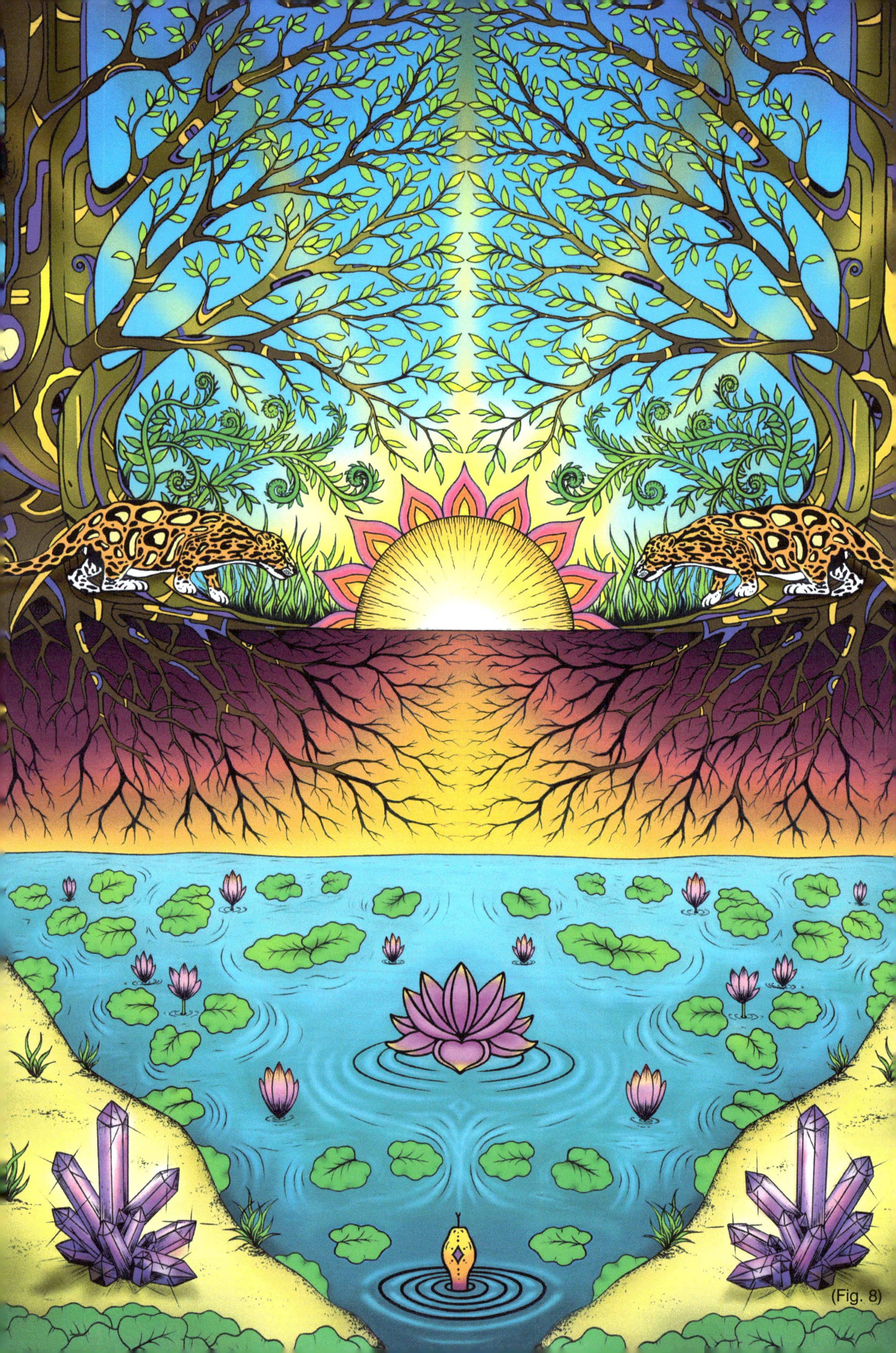

(Fig. 8)

Masterclass 5: Colouring Forest Cats.

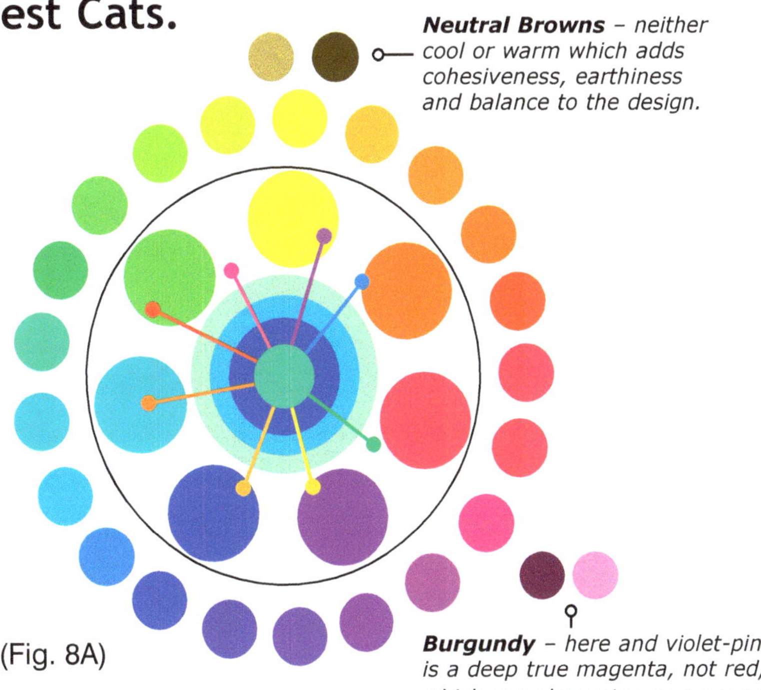

(Fig. 8A)

Shading Techniques:

Shading here is more complex, with shades or tones of various hues being blended together or through various shades of adjoining hues on the colour wheel. The main emphasis is on the sky shading which has both an admixture of gradient style blues, yet also inter-woven soft yellow rays for the Sun. This brings unique colour contrast and a powerful feel to the image. Then we have aqua blue or turquoise water shading which involves a gradient and subtle shading for the movement or ripples of the water. Finally, the bold shading for the gold and burgundy hues, bring an added depth and intensity to the overall design.

Colour distribution:

Colour distribution here is quite diverse, which helps break up the multitude of hues chosen for specific qualities relevant to the panel's syntax or storyline. The yellow and orange hues are confined largely to the centre third section of the image, with the contrasting blue and turquoise hues distributed evenly above and below. The green hues are then inter-laced evenly throughout the blue sections, again, both above and below. This creates a three-part harmony, as green is the adjoining hue of both blue and gold on the colour wheel – (*Companion colour harmony covering up to 8 steps on the colour wheel). This bring the panel's continuity together in terms of colour symmetry or balance, with the green hues seen to be proportionately warmer (lime) toward the top of the image and somewhat cooler green (emerald) towards the very bottom. Lastly, the deep burgundy is centrally placed in the mix to create dramatic colour tension and brings further intensity into the story depiction, helping to further ground the energies of the jaguar totem.

(Fig. 8B)

Forest Cats - (Fig. 8) - In this panel I went for a nice blend of complementary colours, matching the bright orange of the leopards or jaguars with the rich true blues in the sky above. Then I decided to shift the dynamic a bit and use turquoise and teal colours for the water, which are technically still on the blue side and complement well with orange and golden hues of the sun. The forest cats are here resting on the base of the tree, symbolising the grounded force of the solar energy in its capacity to nourish and sustain life, represented here by the trees. The lotus figures are related to the snake here in that they represent gentle awakening or unfolding of energetic potential. They are coloured pink to symbolise the gentle or new aspect of creativity in relation to our aspirations and the fulfilment of either latent or known desires.

The snake entering the frame at the bottom represents here 'Shakti' – the Cosmic Feminine principle energy, or force of procreative power in the Universe. The diamond on her head represents her resting place in the base chakra and this panel's depiction is associated with the first three chakras or energy centres of the subtle anatomny, in relation to the awakening of creative power. The 5 rings or ripples represent the 5 elements of material creation (Earth, Water, Fire, Air, and Ether), associated with their residing place in the first 5 chakras. However, this image syntax relates mainly to the first 3 energy centres and to the manifestion of the will in association with the activation of personal power. It is a gentle energy, self-empowering and energetic, represented here by the subdued curiosity of the leopards. The colours for the sun are also gently activating, symbolising the energies of the new day and there is a balance of masculine and feminine energies on the whole. The brown and tan tones were added to give earthiness and the crystals are amethyst, to symbolise the gentle or refined transformation of energy. The deep burgundy and dusty pink hues represent integration and the grounding of latent potential as it comes to light or into manifestation, which complement well with the rich vibrant greens.

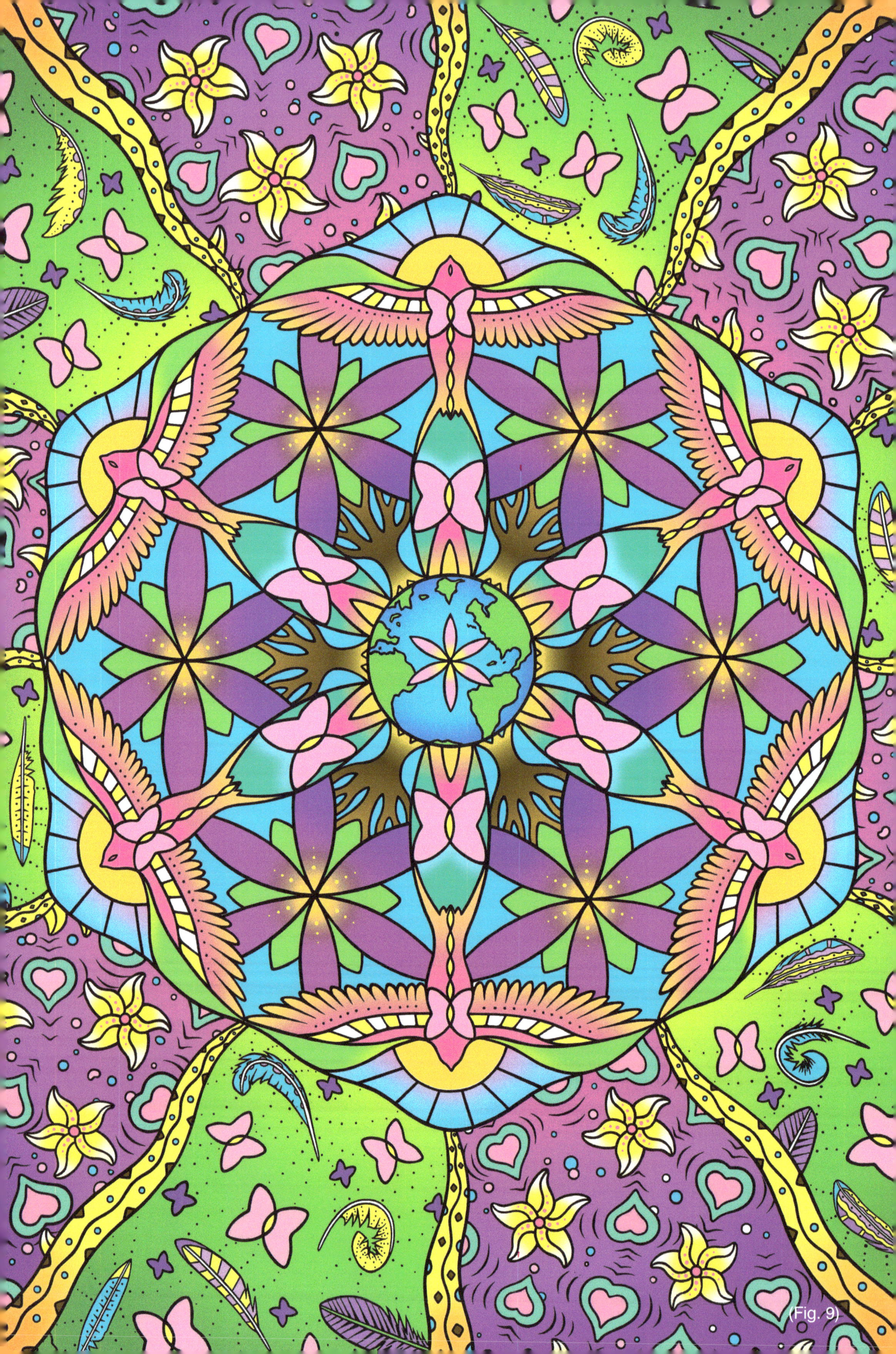

(Fig. 9)

Masterclass 6: Examining Colours for the Swift Mandala.

Shading Techniques:

Colour shading in this panel is mostly for accentuation and the movement of energy to match the storyline, and/or image element depiction. Soft shading on the swifts depicts auspicious energies of the Goddess associated with the early morning and dawn. They also relate to inspiration being sparked, newfound creativity and intuitive growth. The shading on bold yellow elements is to accentuate the principle of illumination and the potential for abundance to be made manifest, expand or grow. Shading on the background further accentuates these principles of expansion/growth, especially in the lime green section. It depicts that the potential for abundance is greatest within, graphically represented by darker shades on the outside and lighter shades within. Shading on the flowers brings further expansion and radial growth potential.

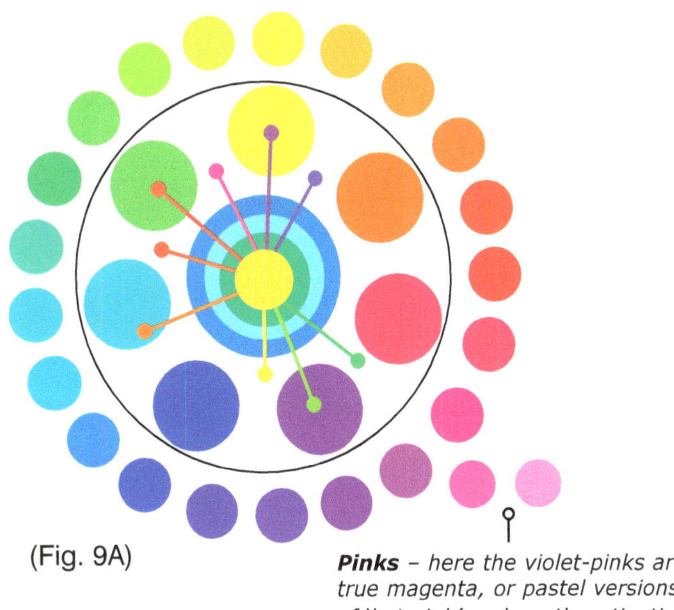

(Fig. 9A)

***Pinks** – here the violet-pinks are true magenta, or pastel versions of 'hot pink' and gently activating.*

Colour distribution:

Colour distribution with this mandala was a bit challenging to achieve the right balance. It is an important mandala depicting a specific Dreamtime storyline and I am more than happy with the results that came through. Abundance for 'World Happiness' and 'World Growth' is clearly depicted by the graphic syntax and placement of image elements, although what would this equate to in terms of colour expression or colour symmetry. The breakdown is complex, yet firstly we have a colour distribution relative to one or two aspects of the Goddess associated with abundance and happiness. This base colour distribution is the 'purple-violet', 'green' and 'gold' hues. Now although these appear to be evenly distributed for convenience, they are in fact quite specific to their placement and elemental association in the image. Finally, soft pinks related to sensitivity to change and openness, which also relate to the Goddess in terms of the energies of Creation associated with inspiration and refined sensitivity. In terms of more practical or 'Earthy' interpretation, the distribution of nature-identical colours are also key to the image having its impact on the material plane and in our physical lives. The impact and syntax translates to: – The trees growing out of the 'Earth', reaching into the 'Heavens' and towards the light of the 'Solar orbs'. The placement and signification of all these colours in association with their image elements allows for final mental assimilation and resolution of the storyline.

(Fig. 9B)

Swift Mandala - (Fig. 9) - Here the colour syntax relatives directly to aspects of the Goddess associated with Abundance and Happiness. Firstly, soft pinks for sensitivity and openness, which also relate to the energies of Creation associated with inspiration and self refinement. I started with the foundational hues of Purple/violet, Pink, Green and Yellow/Gold hues. Colour placement started by deciding on the most obvious hues first, like a blue background for the sky surrounding the birds. Colours for the centre-most element 'Earth' were coloured first and the neutral to warm browns for the trunks of the trees. Then I moved straight into the violet and purple shades of the ellipse flower creation pattern. These were then complemented with green. Now I had the right colours laid down to choose just the right shade and density of sky-blue to be coloured in. Next I thought of ways to accent and contrast with the necessary additions of the golden hues. For the Swift figures I chose here refined pink hues with pastel or soft light yellows for awakening and self renewal. Then a lighter pink tone of the same hue for the butterflies, which also worked great with the complementary green background sections. Gold was certain for the solar discs and coloured next, with the right accents for a twilight shaded sky. Overall, the right amount of green and violet, with gold accent placement illuminating the story in terms of dynamic energy representation. The serpentine figures between the outer background sections were also chosen in the yellow and golden orange hue range to represent further expansion into manifestation. For a similar reason, a golden glow around the Earth was added for abundance and illumination. Yellow flower figures were chosen to complement the violet backing sections and to add expanding spiralling energy, complemented by the soft pink and emerald heart figures. Feathers were coloured to mirror the hues of other image elements, revealing further harmony.

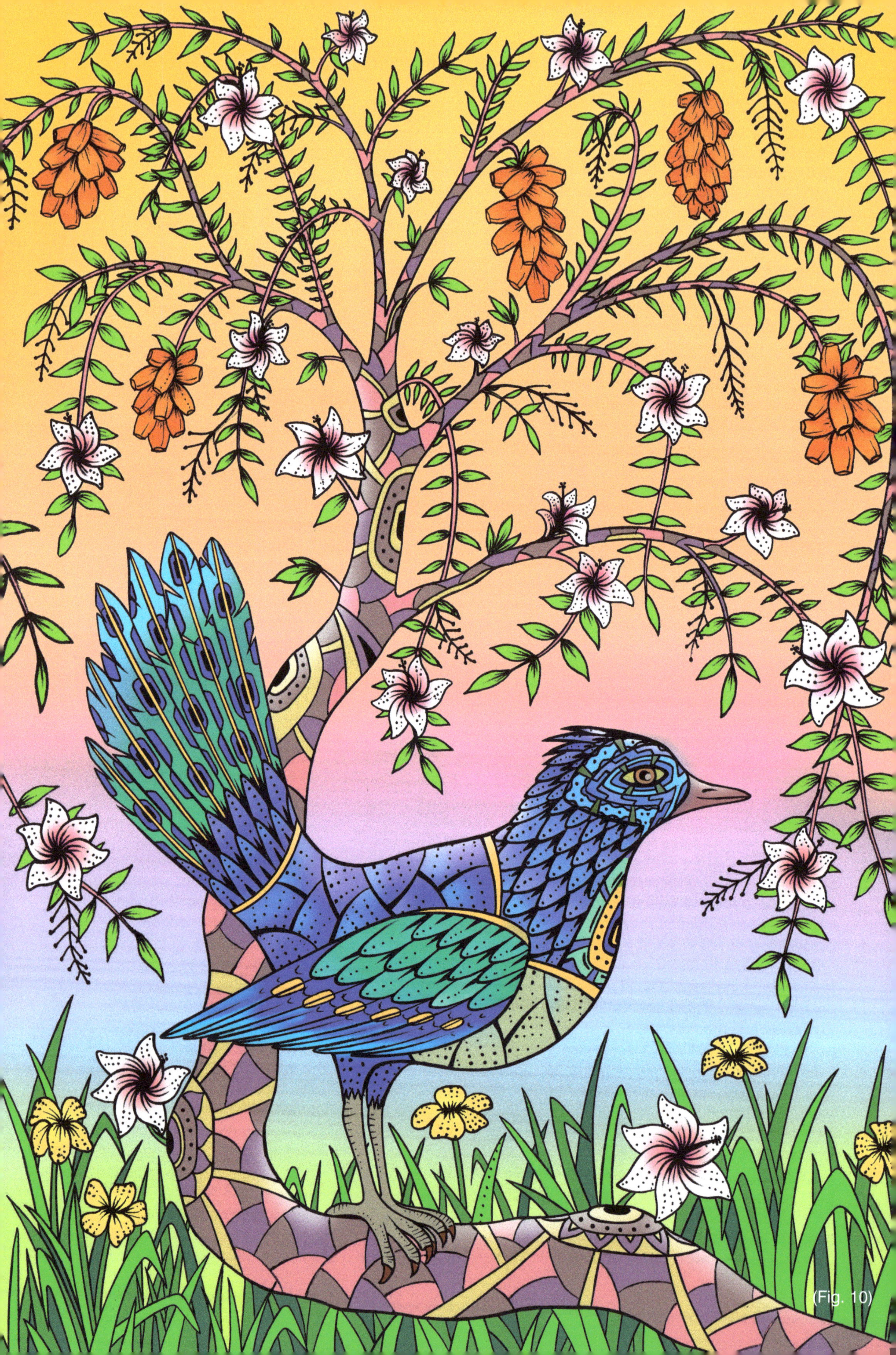

(Fig. 10)

Masterclass 7: Examining Colours for the Forest Wren.

Shading Techniques:

This panel employs a good deal of shading and toning, firstly with the blended admixture of various hues for the sky. Subtle pastel hues were chosen here to complement the overall image balance. Secondly, more subtle accent shading was applied to the wren feathers, employing either neighbouring or complementary hues. There is also some subtle shading on the dusky-pink tree trunk hues. Even if you chose different colours for the tree trunk section, some subtle shading will usually always work well here.

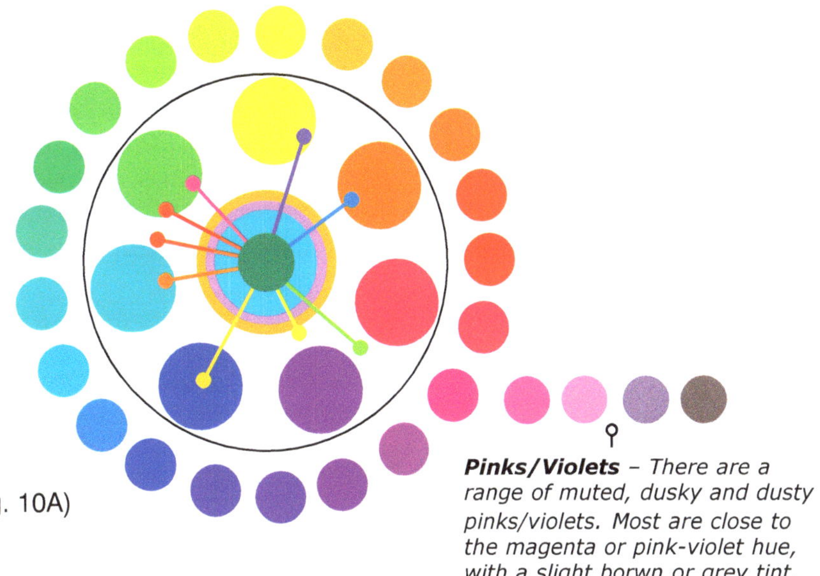

(Fig. 10A)

Pinks/Violets *– There are a range of muted, dusky and dusty pinks/violets. Most are close to the magenta or pink-violet hue, with a slight borwn or grey tint.*

Colour distribution:

Some delightful colour distribution effects are created in this image which is alive with what may be termed bold 'colour symmetry' or refined 'colour harmony'. There is a very invigorating quality achieved by the bright green of the tree leaves and the pastel hues of the sky. The top of the image contains more warm hues, with the bottom exhibiting more cooler aquas and restful blues. The tree trunk mimics the twilight sky with a showcase of dusky pastel pink/ purple hues, mixed with muted dusty pink-browns accented with soft caramel beige. On the whole, not hues one would think to arrange together at first thought and this is often the key to creating truely unique and enlivening art pieces. As the wren is a songbird, I thought it suitable to think of this colour scheme as a music score, symphony or song. To first lay down the right balance of necessary colour notes, accented with enlivening colour harmonies and finished off with a bold crescendo of colour. If you think about it, colour exists as light frequency bands or wavelengths of sound, measurable on the Hertz frequency scale in cycles per second. Coloured light becomes like a wash of musical notes at a rate of measureable or metered sound. So to play with colour is like playing with sound, just like the guitarist lays down a 'riff' – the singer searches for a melodius 'hook', while the bass player seeks to bust out a 'groove' and the drummer secures it all in a 'ryhthm', 'beat', or time signature. Wise or impactful colour distribution then becomes like a good song, or mix in a sense of arranging and recording. The wren represents the crescendo here against a five-part harmony of the twilight sky. The flower tones represent a middle harmony or anchoring centre pitch.

(Fig. 10B)

Forest Wren (Fig. 10) - Alive with colour vitality - the overall appeasing effect is due largely to the predominance of turquoise, aqua and blue of the wren and the complementary greens of the leaves. Further complementary balance is achieved with the contrasting pink, violet and orange sky tones, along with the pastel mocha and dusky-pink accent hues on the tree trunks. Colours were added in a complementary and progressive manner. As you do more and more colouring panels a kind of colour intuition arises by where you attempt to attune to, or feel the colour vibration most necessary or in need. In this vein, try to think of colours being as much frequencies of reflected or harnessed light as they are base or solid pigments. I utilise this 'progressive complementary' or additive colouring approach for most of my colouring, which involves intuitive listening, contemplating and going over various colour admixtures, contrasts or complements in your mind and musing a little on the range of possibilities. Take your time contemplating if a colour doesn't feel quite right and even test colours on a seperate piece of paper before committing to colouring in on the actual art panel, as colours cannot be erased. Ink pens are even less forgiving, whereas pencil choices can be blended and shaded.

There is an important and impactful degree of vibrancy in this panel provided by the lime green accents and yellow elements, which keeps the overall image in the enlivening and activating hue side of the spectrum. The lime green hue is associated with new life potential as we see in nature with seedlings, new shoots, grass or leaves. This colour also gives dynamic contrast in the leaves of the tree with the harmonious sky hues. Then just a hint of saffron and yellow hues to really lift the overall image and give a colour-boost to the psyche. These hues remind us of the radiating warmth and life-giving potential of the Sun. Lastly we have the sky, which brings an invigorating harmony of pastel hues, yet at the same time finishing at the top with a defined amber or golden-yellow cast.

Masterclass 8: Colouring Dynamics For Forest Birds.

In this masterclass we will look at a variety of colour choices for some woodland birds. Like all arenas, there are firstly nature-identical colouring options. There are also key colour qualities that resonate well with the natural energetic signature or totemic values associated with that same creature. This may be for direct practical application or more esoteric in its association or nature. In this masterclas I have chosen a combination of both. In addition to the specific qualities below, refer to Masterclass 10 for totemic colours and Masterclass 11 on general colour qualities, along with the individual panel text for a more diverse application of colour choices.

Hummingbird

This totem often calls for bold and flashy colours in general. You could use pastel tones of a variety of hues, but here I went for strong vivid colours. The violet hues are shaded into purple, which provides the perfect contrast to the bold yellow base body colour. Where the purples become deep and cool, I lightened them up with the invigorating turquoise blue, both shaded, and as solid colour tips to the feathers. Lastly, the yellow was reinforced with further stylised dot markings.

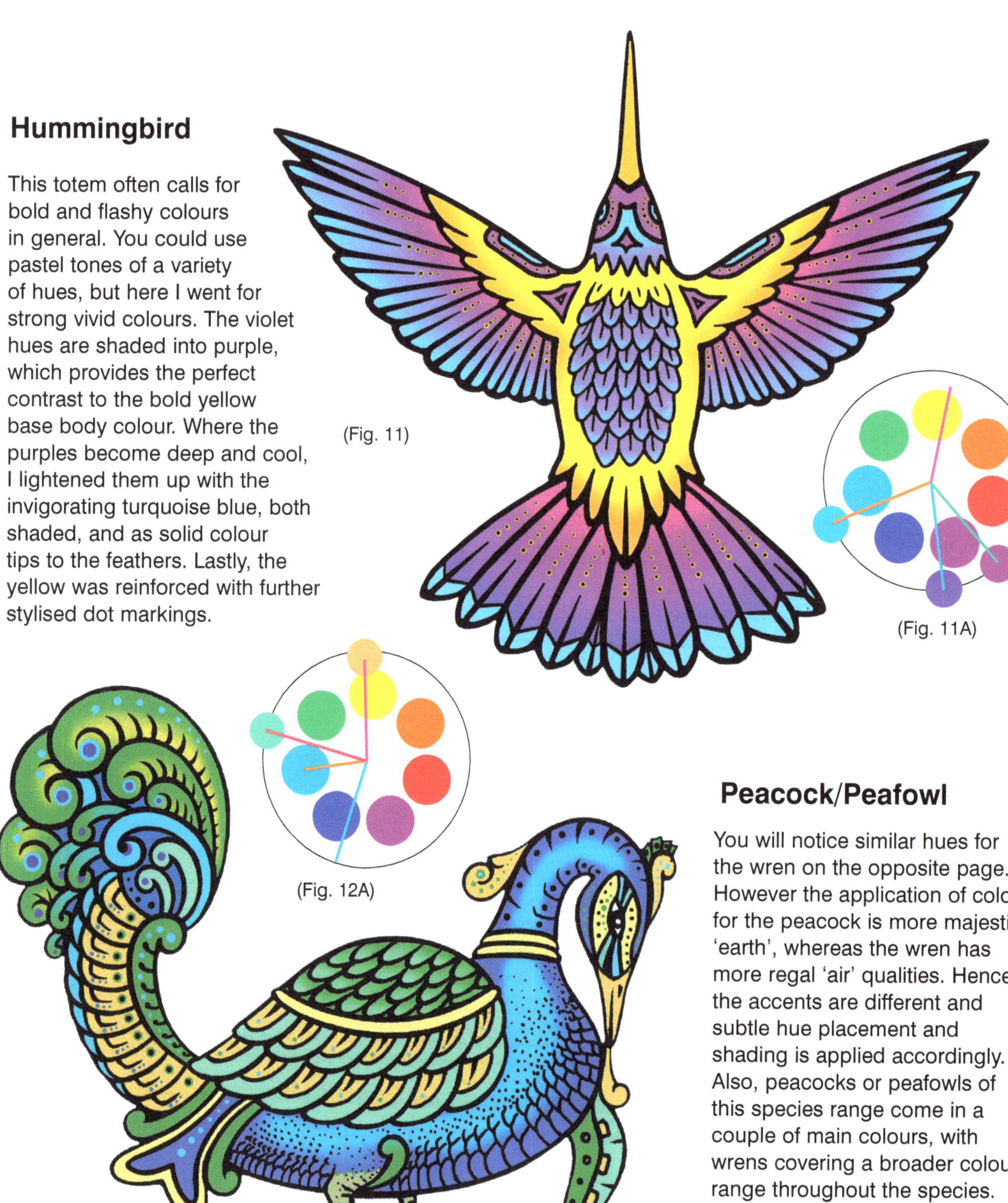

(Fig. 11)

(Fig. 11A)

(Fig. 12A)

(Fig. 12)

Peacock/Peafowl

You will notice similar hues for the wren on the opposite page. However the application of colour for the peacock is more majestic 'earth', whereas the wren has more regal 'air' qualities. Hence, the accents are different and subtle hue placement and shading is applied accordingly. Also, peacocks or peafowls of this species range come in a couple of main colours, with wrens covering a broader colour range throughout the species. Reference colour photos from the internet on peacocks for further inspiration and examples.

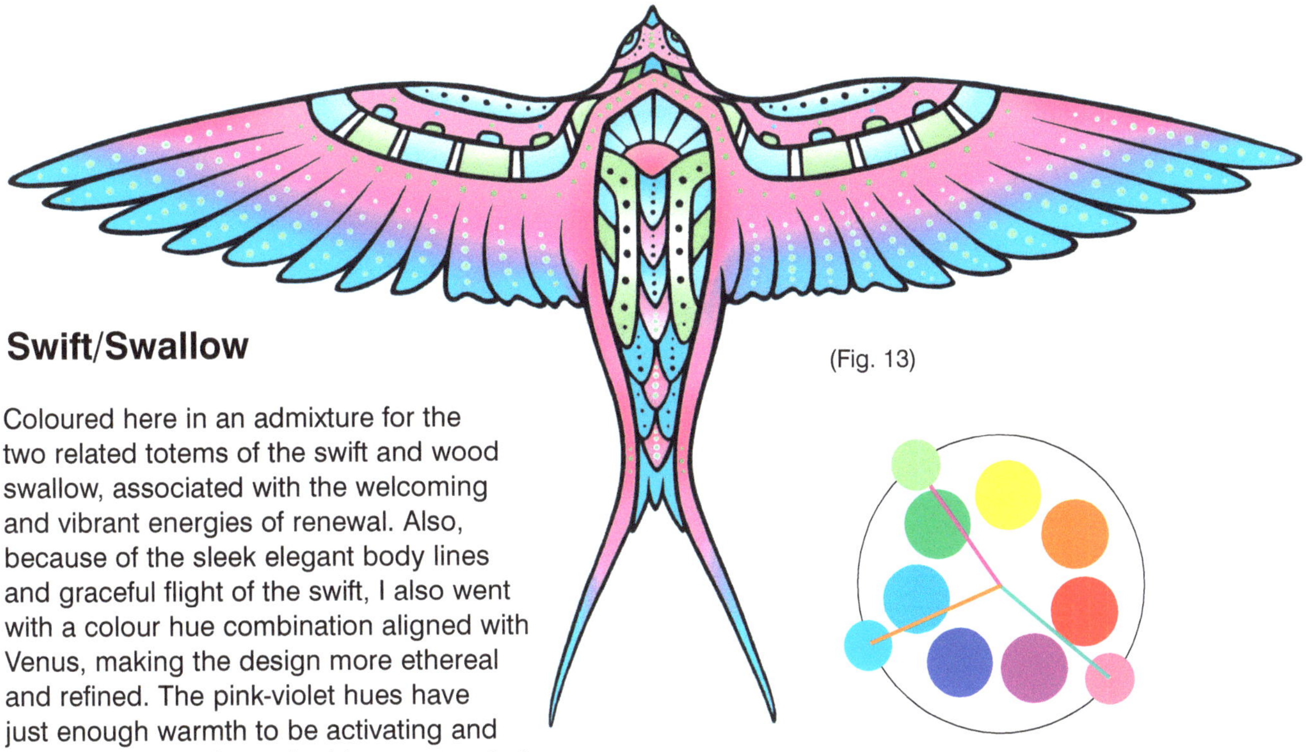

Swift/Swallow

(Fig. 13)

Coloured here in an admixture for the two related totems of the swift and wood swallow, associated with the welcoming and vibrant energies of renewal. Also, because of the sleek elegant body lines and graceful flight of the swift, I also went with a colour hue combination aligned with Venus, making the design more ethereal and refined. The pink-violet hues have just enough warmth to be activating and the turquoise and powder blues somewhat neutral, or slightly invigorating. The apple green hues are soft and interwoven with white to give further variegation.

(Fig. 13A)

Observation*: When choosing pastels, often the colour density needs to be just right to suit the artwork or image. I went for mid-density pastels above, or slightly on the lighter side of mid pastel colours in some shaded areas. However if this colour combination was chosen for a colouring panel or artwork I would factor in the size of the bird and the overal placement of the bird as an image element, to get the right colour balance or appropriate feel.*

Wren/Songbird

As wrens are bold and regal birds, colours where chosen to highlight these qualities. Bold royal blue shaded with turquoise and emerald hues worked well. Then, final highlighting with vivid saffron gold really picks up the colour dynamic in a way that is aligned with the bird's characteristic traits and totemic signature. Similar colour dynamics can be chosen with other related robins and songbirds, with some deep or defined base colours hilighted or complemented with a variety of contrasting colours. It is often best to aim for 3 to 4 colours or hue bands, unless it is a bird species given to more colour variegation, such as some parrots and or hummingbird.

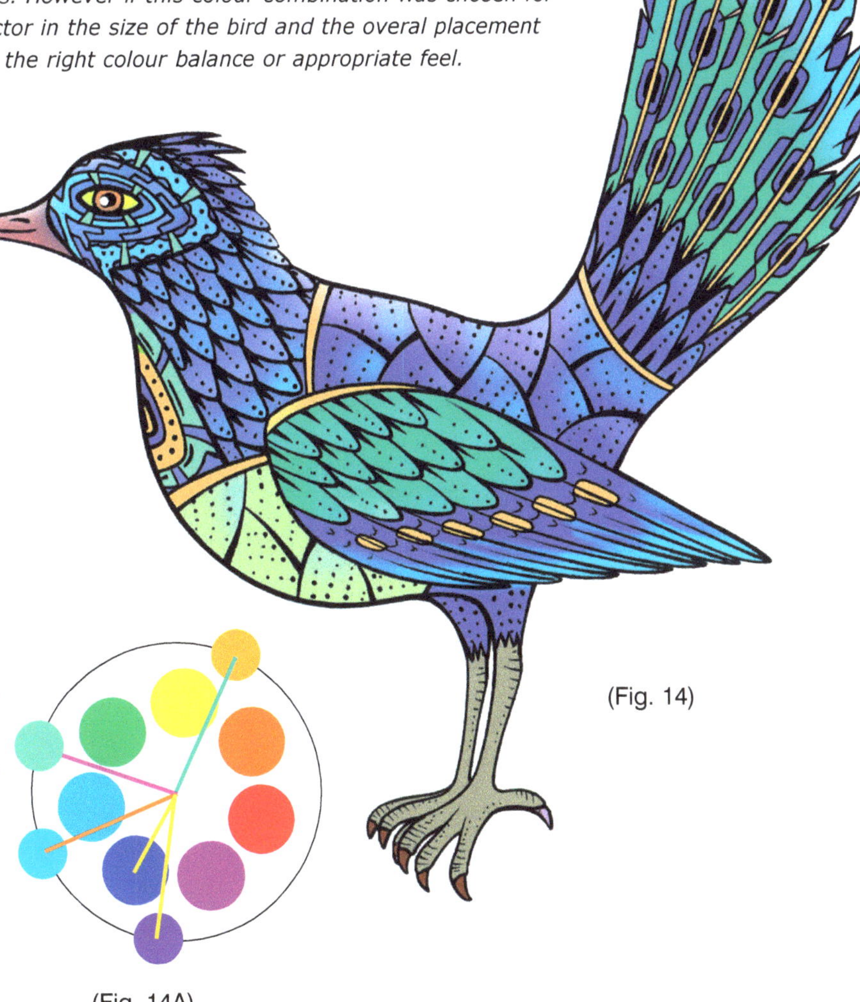

(Fig. 14)

(Fig. 14A)

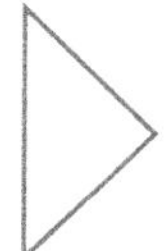

The hummingbird totem is associated with the capacity for celebration and multi-faceted expression of the heart. Hummingbird energy is reflected in the wide-eyed and carefree smile of a child. It represents at times an uncompromising appreciation for freedom and being beyond the grasp of things that worry or burden our lives or that may otherwise weight heavy on the human heart. For with joy comes appreciation and through appreciation gratitude is deepened and more happiness acquired. Hummingbirds have iridescent colours that are enlivened or intensified in bright light. There is an aspect of this totem that almost demands we seek greater light and a fuller expression of life, with this characteristic being represented by their shimmering multi-faceted or rainbow hues. Colours for this image are detailed in Masterclass 3, although this is just one example, as this panel lends itself to many colour combinations and can be seen as one of the most experimental in the book.

People with hummingbird as a totem have a dislike for oppressive energies in the world. They abhor any kind of bondage or enslavement to unnecessary responsibility, espicially the kind that is dictated, asigned, or measured out by others. These are the types who would rather live as a free spirit with little food or money, rather than to be bound by the world and burdened by levels of responsibility that eat at the very core or concept of what it means to have freewill. This energy can be relentless in its own right and cause hummingbird people to need to be carefree or unattached in relationships at times, even if this feels uncomfortable, unnatural or against the grain. However, it is more a case of being free from controlling or manipulating relationship dynamics, whether they be in the work arena or in their personal relationships. Likewise, free from burdensome restrictions like a heavy mortgage, or the modern day '12 insurance policy' mindset or model.

The hummingbird's joy shines light on where and why we feel despair at times with uncompromising intensity. It shares that happiness and fulfilment are not birthrights, yet more like decisions that at times need to be made to remove us from ignorance and restriction in life. In this regard, our sense of self limitation becomes lighter, freer and more in line with what will bring true joy and sustained freedom, not mere pleasure fulfilment associated with superficial or temporal happiness. If in doubt for colour choices, be sure to include signature colours for the hummingbird's characteristic qualities like yellow and violet. Otherwise colour freely in variegated hues or a multi-faceted colour scheme that serves the hummingbird's iridescent play of colour and lively dynamic appeal.

A stereographic panel, which is very helpful for a more mediattive colouring journey and attaining greater equillibrium between the left and right hemispheres of the brain, as well as integration between the masculine and femmine aspects of the psyche. The forest flowers have a somewaht tropical feel, with this panel representing balancing energetics, like when we are in a tropical paradise with the water close to the same temperature as the warm air. This panel also has some association with the twilight and spring junctures of nature, which also bring a feeling of newfound joy and being free from restrictions. The fruits and seedpods at the bottom represent the fruits of our attainment, through which without, we often have little or no cause for joy. Hence, they could be coloured in one of your favourite colours. or colours that represent joy, celebration and the attainment of your goals. The base of the image has a lotus (renewal) and watercourse which brings the life-sustaining water into what is otherwise a very 'earthy' and 'airy' panel. *For further colour analysis, see page 13.

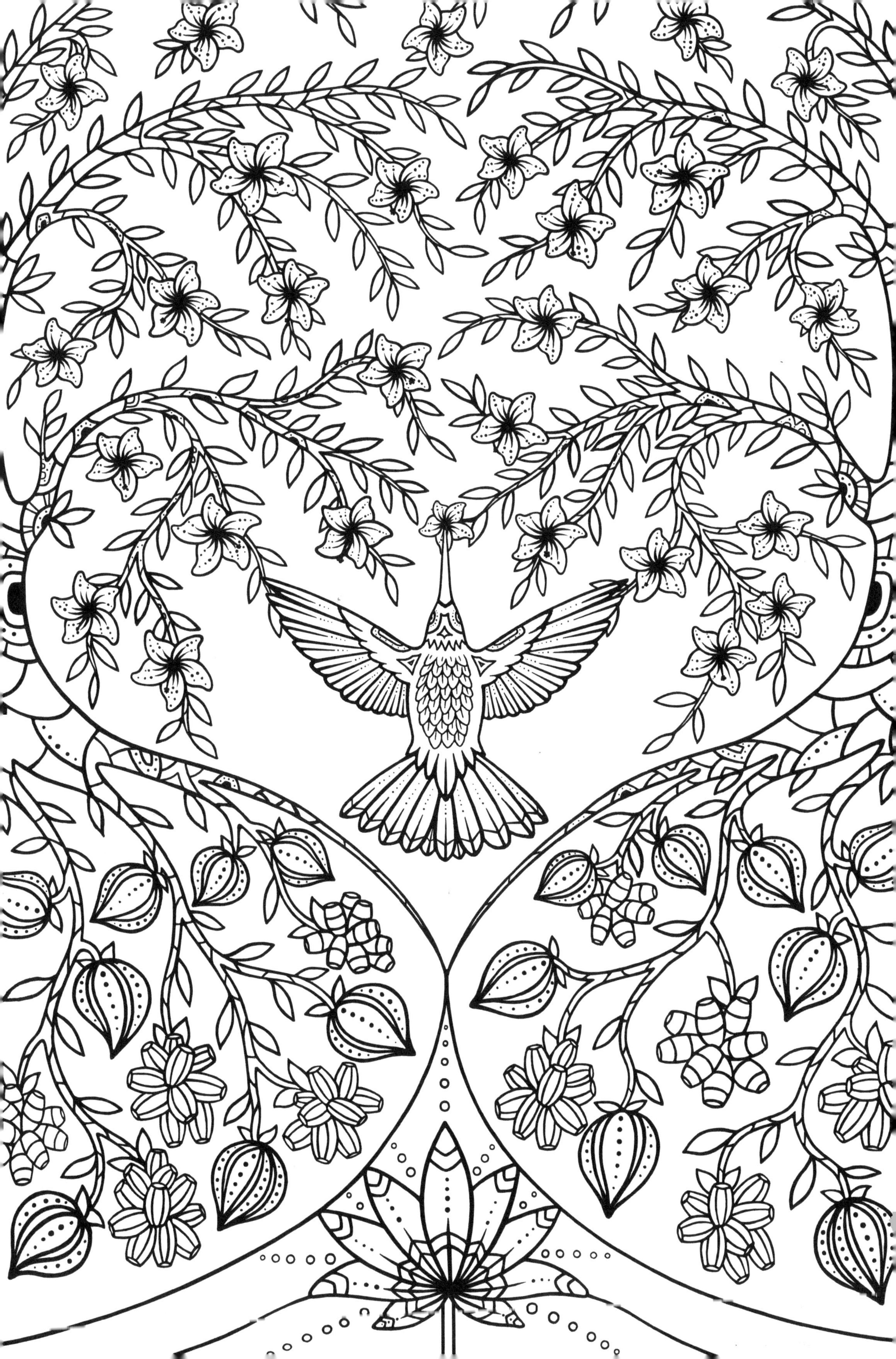

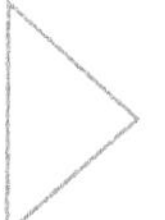

The squirrel totem is traditionally associated with making more time for play and joy in our life. Take time out from our burdens or busy schedule, to make time for curious and experiential activities and passtimes. These can often be things we have put off through lack of time, with squirrel medicine being remedial for the modern 'time-poor' world, which eats away at our innate curiosity, sense of innocense, the very spitit of adventure and the essential need at times to 'just play'. It is also associated with focused attention for future plans and goals. In this panel the squirrel represents the energies of spring, with new growth, spring flowers and swifts darting around, accentuating this panel's association with freedom and joy. There is a clear sense of innocence and youthful vigour in the combined symbology of the image. The small butterfly figures represent ever-new transformation and symbolise newfound vitality associated with the morning energies of the sun.

Colours associated with this dynamic are light golden yellows, lime greens and warm earthy browns. Violet and hot pink hues would work well with the butterflies and spring flowers as they are also associated with the swift totem, in its association to receive the vitalising and activating warmth of the Sun. To colour them as related wood swallows, colours like indigo, lavender and electric blue may suit, to symbolise welcoming energetics and letting go of the past in association with elements of conflict, burden, suffering or distress. For this dynamic, maybe shift the sky colour away from a light sky blue to better contrast or accentuate the bird and butterfly figures. Indigo shaded sections with blue, a twilight, or even an early morning sky might work well with pinks and oranges.

Together the combined totems of the butterfly, squirrel and the swift/swallow symbolise welcomeness, domestic happiness, and moving beyond the worries, burdens or insecurities of the past. These are the limitations that limit or deny our happiness, that shackle or plague us with wrong thinking, dependency or despair. The salmon figures represent the principle of 'abundance' that is attained through nourishing that which matters most for our fulfilment and sense of joy. The image is designed to bring in more home happiness and domestic peace and to move through negative restrictions or turmoil with a renewed sense of optimism or faith. The colours suggested serve this aim, yet you could just as easily choose colours that are most suited to your personal colouring journey, as this is meant to be a light-hearted and vibrant colouring panel overall.

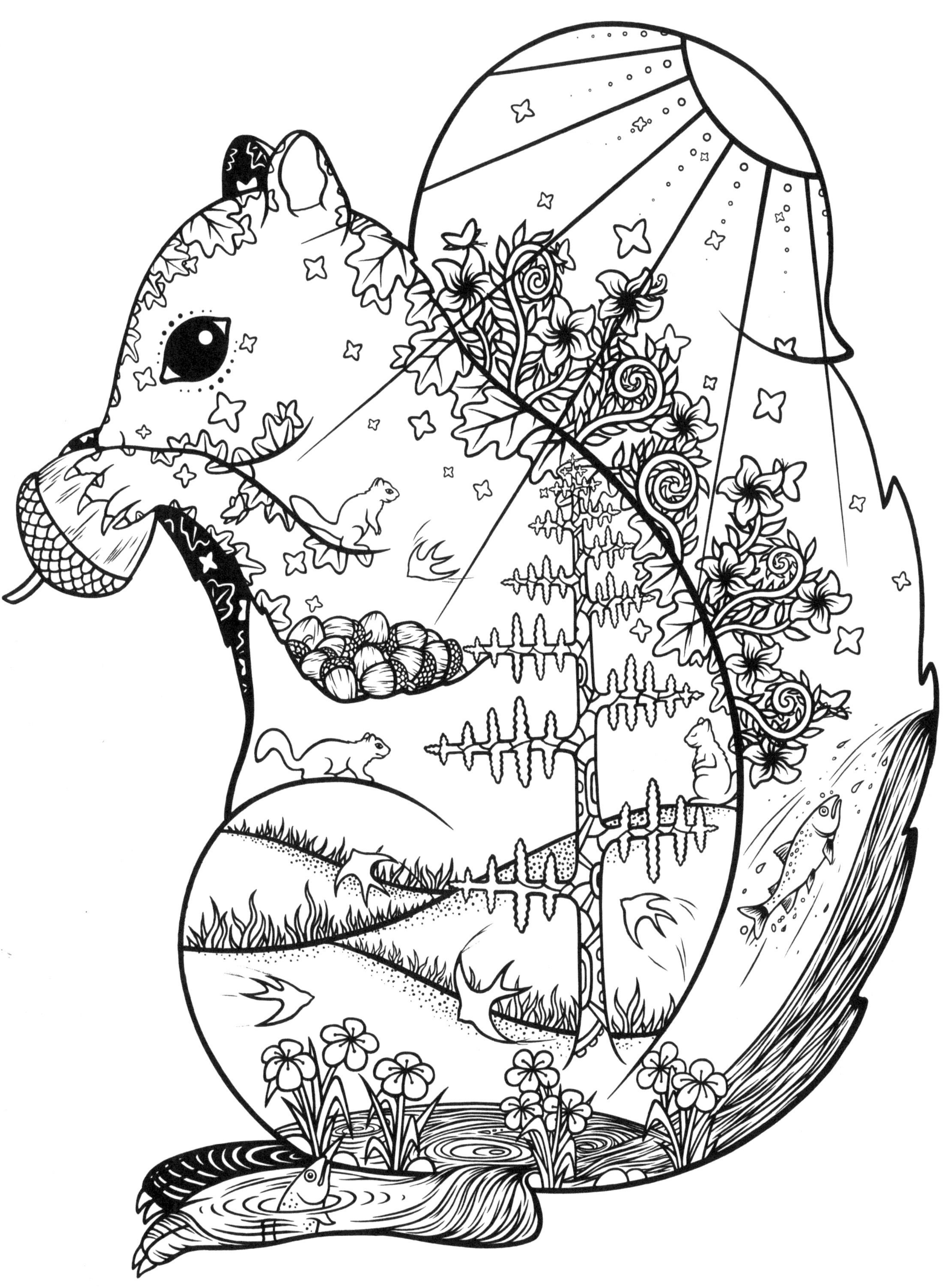

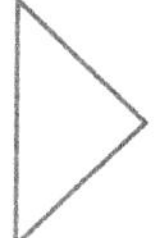

Dragonflies relate to the power of light, multidimensionality, enchantment and the mythical fairy realms. Associated with magical occurrences, the dragonfly totem relates to the very energetic interrelationship between creativity and new dimensions of reality coming into the physical or material world. Although related somewhat to the butterfly in association with regenerative powers, dragonfly energy is more specifically about the principle of flux and change in the process of creative vision and the creative force that fuels our desires. It is not an earth totem, though it does have an association with materialisation and what we bring into being, with, or through material elements of/in the physical plane. It is more related to the 'air' element, having also some direct elemental association with water, as water like a mirror reflects the interrelationship of the very 'play of light'.

Dragonfly energy teaches us to be mindful of own sense of illusion that we project on or into the material world. Self truth and self illusion are intimately connected and the dragonfly shares that our inner light of perception defines our self truth. The kind of innate truth that exists veiled beyond the objects that 'light' temporally illumines or presents to be satisfying or fulfilling in our outer physical world. We can see how light gives body and defines shape, yet it also enlivens our desires and fascinations through its association with how we perceive objects and environments in the material world. Dragonfly energies guide us to be more aware of our powers of perception that relate to what we are creating and defining with light in our very lives. So it denotes the potential for multifaceted awareness and self truth, or the pitfalls of illusion and us seeing only what the ego wants us to see.

The dragonfly relates to multi-colour and variegated hues, especially pastel hues of the cool and neutral colours like aqua, pastel blue, lilacs and soft pastel violets. They can be used to connect to the magical fairy realms and the dragonfly totem used in the place of more menacing dragon figures symbolically, which of course represent somewhat deeper, more powerful or dark totemic energies. Dragonfly still wields great power and the totem needs to be respected in regards to the potential illusion and change it can accentuate or initiate in our lives. The blindside for the dragonfly totem is insatiable or self-perpetuated desires, along self-limiting behavioural aspects or traits that become self-delusional, preventing us from a shift in consciousness that would otherwise encourage personal growth and natural self development. The dragonfly totem is reflective of these traits, which can at times be confronting. Part of its totemic potential is to do with the very dissolution of illusion and with the self-generating and regenerating power of creativity, new light and opportunities into our life.

Colours for the specific setting may be to utilise water colours of any blue and aqua hues for the background, where shading and blending would convey further movement of energies. Then the lotus figures could be complemented with gold and soft pinks or soft violets. Check colour combinations for actual dragonflies on the internet, as they come in all manner of hues and colour banding styles. This totem is more suited to lighter or pastel colours than intense deep or dark ones in general, however bold colours like violet, yellow and vivid turquoise can work well as accents.

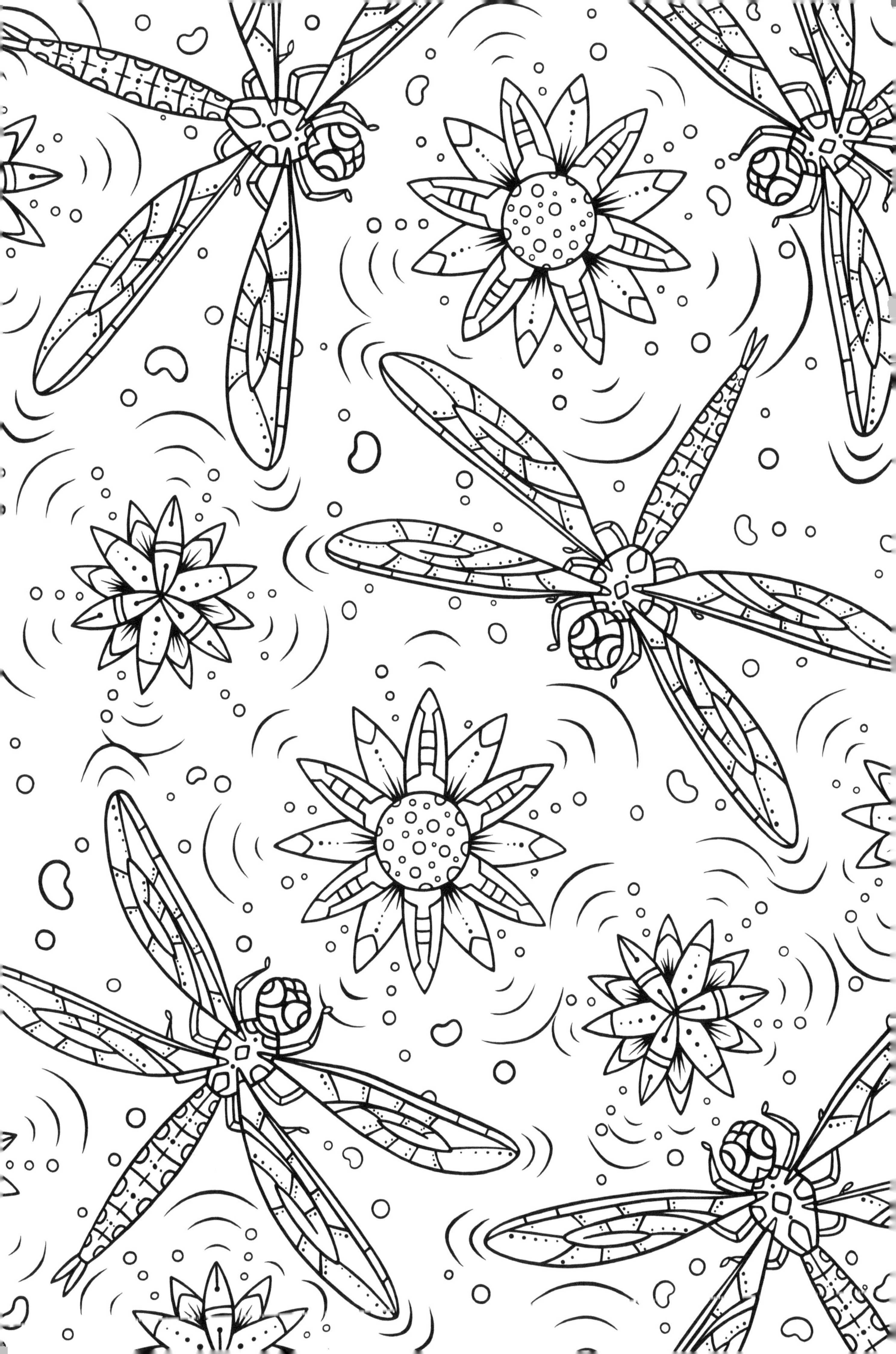

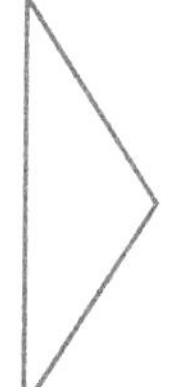

This panel conveys the lighthearted joyous energetics of Spring. The forest deer is an enigmatic and gentle totem with lunar sensibilities. Often associated with the Moon in its role with sensitivity to energy, the cycles of nature and forest magic in legends and folklore. Here we have a clear solar panel expression, with spring flowers, fresh foliage and the hummingbirds fluttering free. Hummingbirds are associated with the very spirit of joy, the freedom of spirit that exists unburdened or unrestricted by the outer world by any major degree. Colours for the hummingbirds can be pretty much any colour that suits your rendition of the storyline of freedom and the joy of spring. What I often find best with a panel like this is to colour the green foliage first and maybe the Solar orb gold or orange. This way we have a foundation laid to complement colours for the other elements.

For example, green and gold would then work well with violet of purple for the hummingbirds, or you could choose to blend these hues with the 'already chosen' yellow or green in the hummingbirds wings or body features. For the butterfly figures, either choose colours that work well for the totem in its association with transformation and renewal. like soft pinks, hot pink or violet tones, Alternatively, any colour that suits your artistic rendition, as even yellow would bring defining or accentuating effects once the other hues are coloured in to complement. The larger tree is a stylised 'magnolia tree', associated with timeless appreciation and the joy of unconditional or all-enduring love, so maybe choose colours that resonate well with these qualities for you. The spring flowers can be in any colour, yet what often works well is to leave them, or the butterflies until last, this way they can then complement the other colours best and really bring the overall sense of colour symmetry alive.

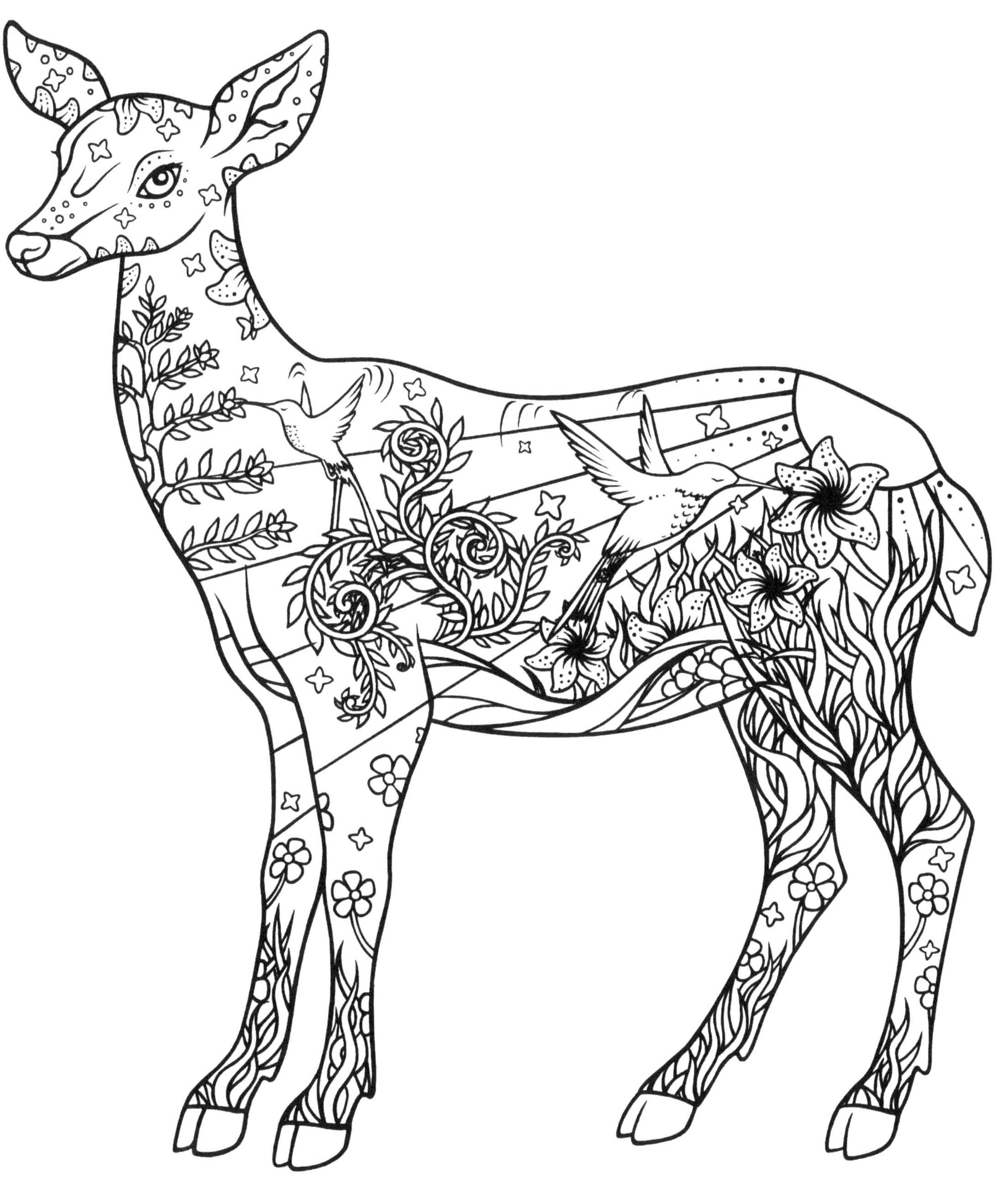

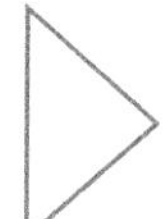

This hummingbird panel is alive with colouring potential and full of symbology and syntax to further creativity and inspiration. We have 3 defined domains of Earth, Water and Air. These could be utilised to compartmentalise your colouring options somewhat. For example, one way to go about colouring would be to start with blue water. The specific hue of the water may need to be relative to the sky colour. If you wanted a true light sky blue for example. You may choose to make the water and aqua blue or somewhat contrasting with the sky to seperate the domains somewhat, or what you want them to symbollically represent. Maybe indigo elements would work well by shading the water and blending with deeper indigo towards the bottom. Alternatively, you may choose a twilight sky or an orange and gold sunset blend. In any case, it often helps to muse over the colour options like this to some degree before committing and starting to colour.

The hummingbird totem itself relates to the variegation of colour and a multidimensional approach, so keep this in mind and its association with the principles of joy and freedom of spirit. The fish here represent abundance and creativity in its fluid and fertile state. Any colours for the fish may suit and it is one way to make the panel dynamic and visually impacting, so maybe choose their colours last or towards the end for full effect. The flowers are in the tropical 'hibiscus' or 'frangipani' style, reminiscent of locations like 'Hawaii', 'The Caribbean' or 'The Bahamas'. So you can make these bold and colourful, otherwise I find yellow, gold-orange, violet or hot pink works well when colouring just the centres and leaving some white towards the edge for a feeling of openness. Alternatively, use two tones, like a violet centre with yellow tips, or the other way around. Other than these suggestions, just be creative and follow your sense of colour intuition. Where the image works well with a predominance of bright and vibrant colours like lime greens, vivid aquas, yellow, orange and violet, it can just as easily accomodate soft pinks, beige and tan hues. Deep, dark or even turbulent odd admixtures for the catfish at the bottom can work. Browns, burgundy hues or tawny greens mixed with plum, purple or grey tones comes to mind – the choice is yours.

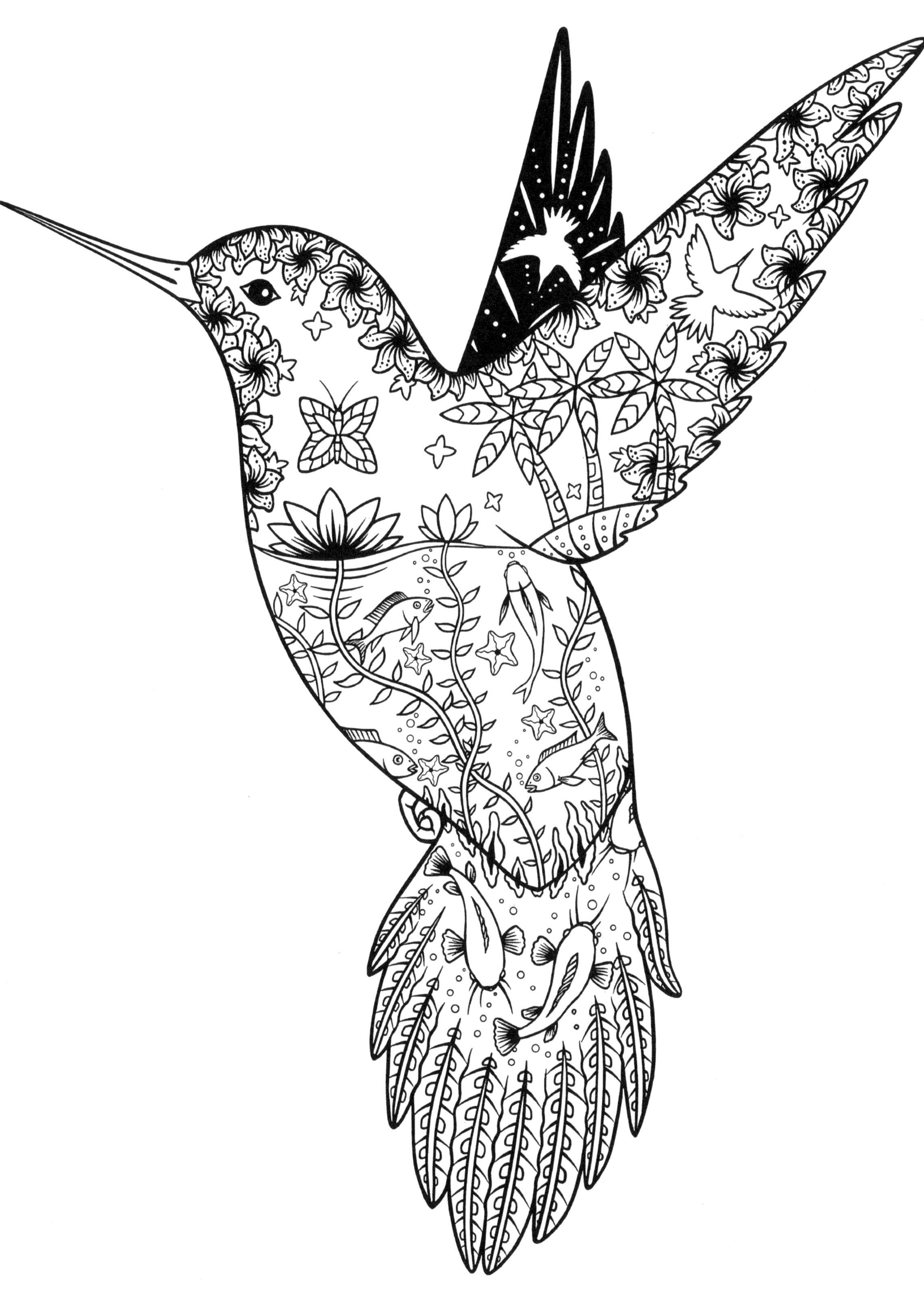

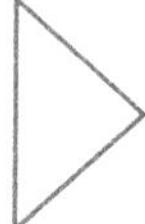

This image depicts the forest 'Winter' months, with pine fronds and stylised snowflakes floating freely in wind. Colours ideally should be on the cool side, however one could just as easily colour in any colour combination. One example would be to utilise some colours that are somewhat off distinct true colour hues, like 'pine-green' – defined as a deep cool-green with a touch of black or dark brown in it. Also, one might choose a dark 'Prussian blue' or 'Phthalo blue' for the background, which are blues with the addition of some black, or often so heavily pigmented that they appear dark. These two blues are generally dark, yet often slightly on the green-blue or purple-blue side of true neutral dark blue. Likewise, brown hues can be used for the tree branches or even silver-greys mixed with highlights or accent colours along the branch segments. You could even try actual silver inks, which would contrast well with deep blue sky. These are just some examples to make this panel outside the norm of just applying more standardised true colours. The stylised snowflake elements are really to give interesting colouring options and if you chose the 'off-true colours' suggested above for the backgrounds elements, then you are often in a clearer space to chose distinct workable or more pleasing colours for the snowflakes. Otherwise, soft pastels of various colour and hue combinations would work well, maybe mixed in with some darker hues reflecting from the background colours. Colour shading will also work very well with the snowflakes.

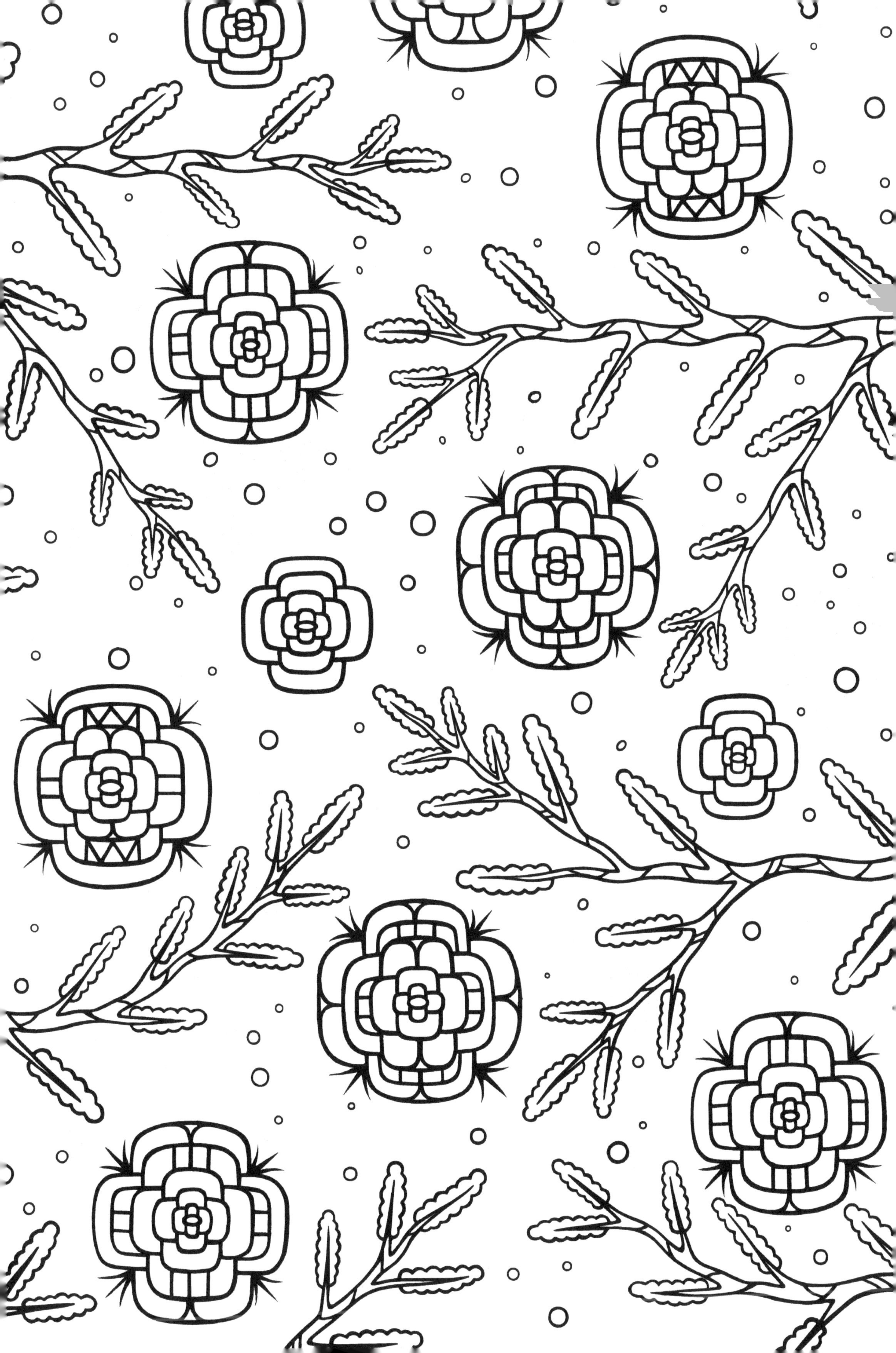

Masterclass 9: Colouring Forest Flowers and Trees.

Masterclass 9 ventures into the colourful world of forest flowers. Colour examples here are often contrasting and dynamic, however feel free to experiment with the softer colour combinations of more pastel hues.

Lotus and Water lily blooms can often be coloured soft pink or a more mid to deep magenta hue. They can also have shaded, blushed or highlighted tips on an otherwise white bloom, which contrasts well with the saffron yellow bud centre. There are also blue and indigo varieties, yet these are usually modern hybrids, or confused with the Egyptian blue water lily. Water lilies come in a wider range of hues and I like to include them in most water ponds and lagoons for added colour and symbolic effect. Here I have gone for a nice violet/magenta/gold admixtures, accented with the aqua and green water colours of the pond setting.

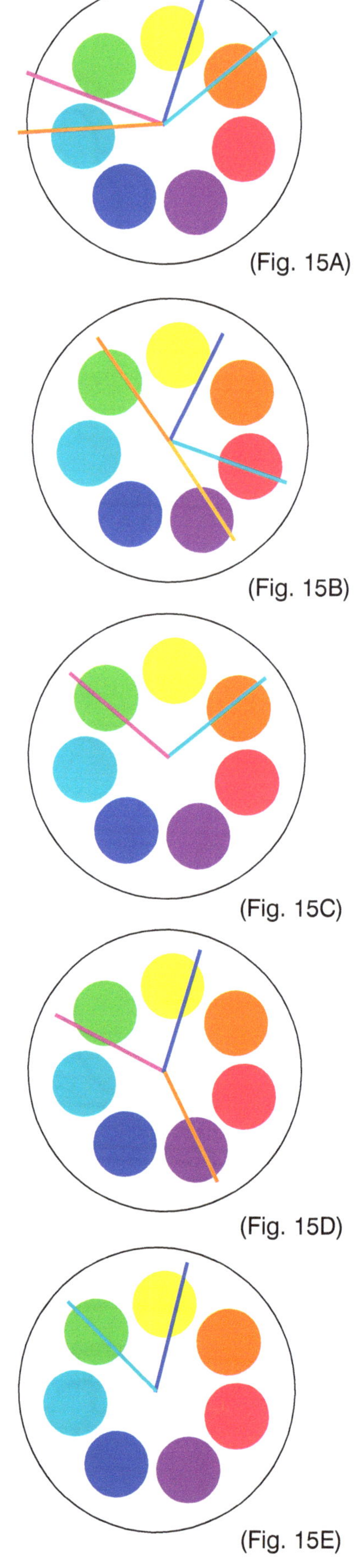

(Fig. 15A)

Cherry Blossoms come in pink and white, or 'pink blushed', with some interesting effects that can really lighten up an artwork or panel. What I went for here is a soft and variegated combination of hues, involving the banded tree branch graphics to display a more subtle hue combination. Pink complements well with green, but as there are no green foliage at the point of cherries blossoming, I added the soft pastel apple green hues in here for contrast and effect. If simplifying the design, just try soft pinks and pastel greens, which often work well by themselves. Alternatively, try any two other colours of choice with the pink blush effect.

(Fig. 15B)

Tiger Lilies come in a variety of colours in nature. Here I chose bright saffron and bright orange hues, which complement well with the green background foliage of nature scenes. Tiger lilies also lend themselves well to colour shading or toning. One example would be to leave them white and shade just the centres similar to the hibiscus examples below. However, this technique looks better if the shading is a stripe to accentuate the tiger lily centre strip and markings.

(Fig. 15C)

Aurum Lilies have been hybridised in nature as the 'Calla lily', (not to be confused with the 'Canna Lily') which both come in a wide spectrum of rainbow hues. Here I chose the violet/purple colour range and included soft pastel stripes with a subtle shaded throat to the lily. The combination of white with bold violet and pastel purple complements well with the saffron stamen of the lilly. The whole colour combination also works well to provide further colour variegation with green foliage, with the lily leaves here in a nice cool or deep emerald green.

(Fig. 15D)

Spring Flowers I often include in an image to symbolise renewal and the awakening energies of spring. These energetics or image dynamics are well suited to plain bold yellow, the colour of expansion and growth. Here 'yellow' of the spring bulb is highlighted by the sister of brother hue of green on the colour wheel. Green and yellow are not always pleasing colours to use together and are kind of a one-way complementary (yellow complements green, yet green doesn't necessarily complement yellow). However for flowers and leaf/grass combinations they often work well. What often work well is if you shift the green slightly towards the blue, giving an aqua green, and when yellow becomes saffron, even better suited. Alternating flower colours like yellow and violet also works well.

(Fig. 15E)

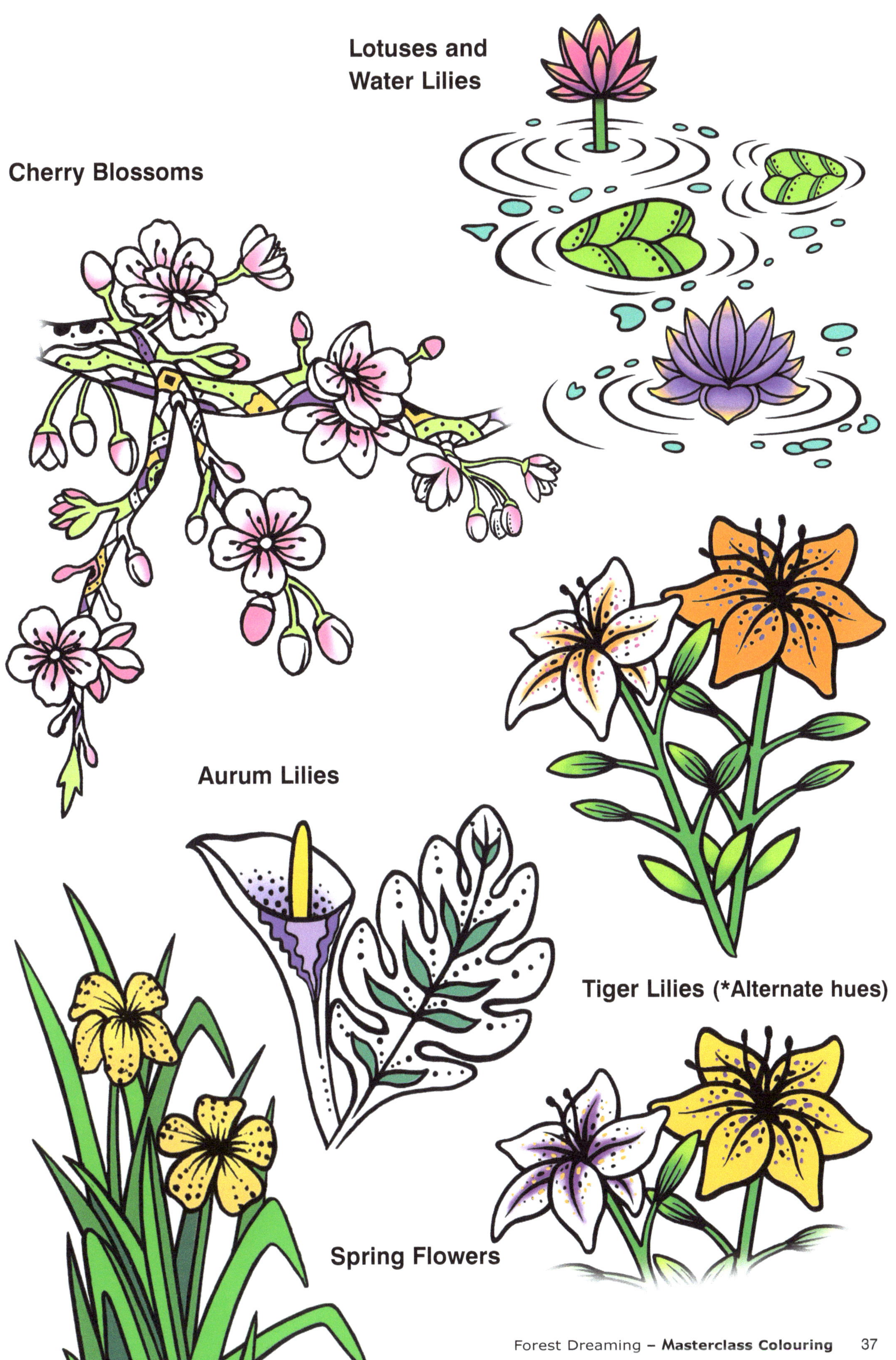
Lotuses and
Water Lilies
Cherry Blossoms
Aurum Lilies
Tiger Lilies (*Alternate hues)
Spring Flowers

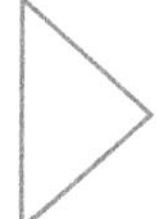

Wolves are powerful, yet misunderstood totems of the canine world. They are often seen as lunar totems associated with the Moon, yet some of the wolf's totemic traits are more solar in nature. This panel shows the awakening and youthful vigour of the wolf, a totem associated with kinship and 'pack' or 'group' loyalty. Wolves are very social animals that value family, community and instinctual knowledge or action. This panel shows a lone wolf calling to the light of the Sun in the early evening Full Moon. In some animal totem circles, cats are considered feminine and to convey 'lunar' sensibilities, whereas dogs or canines are considered masculine or 'solar'. This goes against the stereotypical association of the wolf totem with the Moon. However, in other Dreamtime legends we also see the brother/sister animal; the 'Coyote' associated with solar myths and stories, with dogs found further associated with masculine deities like Shiva in Indian and Tibetan cosmology.

In this panel there are 4 totems – the 'wolf', the 'hawk', the 'butterfly' and the 'swift'. The hawk represents the intuitive capacity or power of visionary potential. Hawks and wolves both have some relation to intuitive messages that are good for the collective, group or community as a whole. They relate in this sense to the planet Mercury, (Buddha, Thoth, Hermes), the messenger and scribe in the Pantheon of the Gods. Hawks are associated with messages from the spirit world or signify celestial messengers in many myths and legends. They relate to clarity of vision, insight and increased awareness or a new-found perspective. The butterflies and swifts in this panel represent the free-spirited nature and innocent play of the forest life that comes alive at sunrise and early morning. They are depicted here as solar totems, or more so, animals that delight in the joy and proliferation of light. The Sun and the Moon represent a seasonal juncture, which is here a Full Moon, or physically Sun/Moon opposition. A solid deep blue or indigo sky may suit, or you could always try a twlight sky with some shading.

Some interesting dynamics and contrasting effects can be attained with this panel, by colouring the solar aspect of the image inside the wolf, with the lunar aspect outside. Maybe try warm greens, golds, pinks and yellows for the solar aspect and then go for cool or neutral greens, blues and cool or neutral browns and tans for the outer image. The stylised glyph patterns of the lower part of the image could be coloured in contrasting hues. This style of graphics often benefits by first choosing 3 to 4 colours and alternating them, yet keeping a good deal of white in the mix. Alternatively a neutral or mid tan brown may also benefit the image by being interwoven here with other cool colours like emerald, indigo, aqua and purple. Green hues can add balance, by being neither warm nor cool as 'emerald green', or bring brightness and vibrancy as 'lime green'. Alternatively, deep cool greens for the pine trees or as an accent hue can bring a sense of calmness of balance to these image sections and work well to bridge or reinforce a cool blue sky.

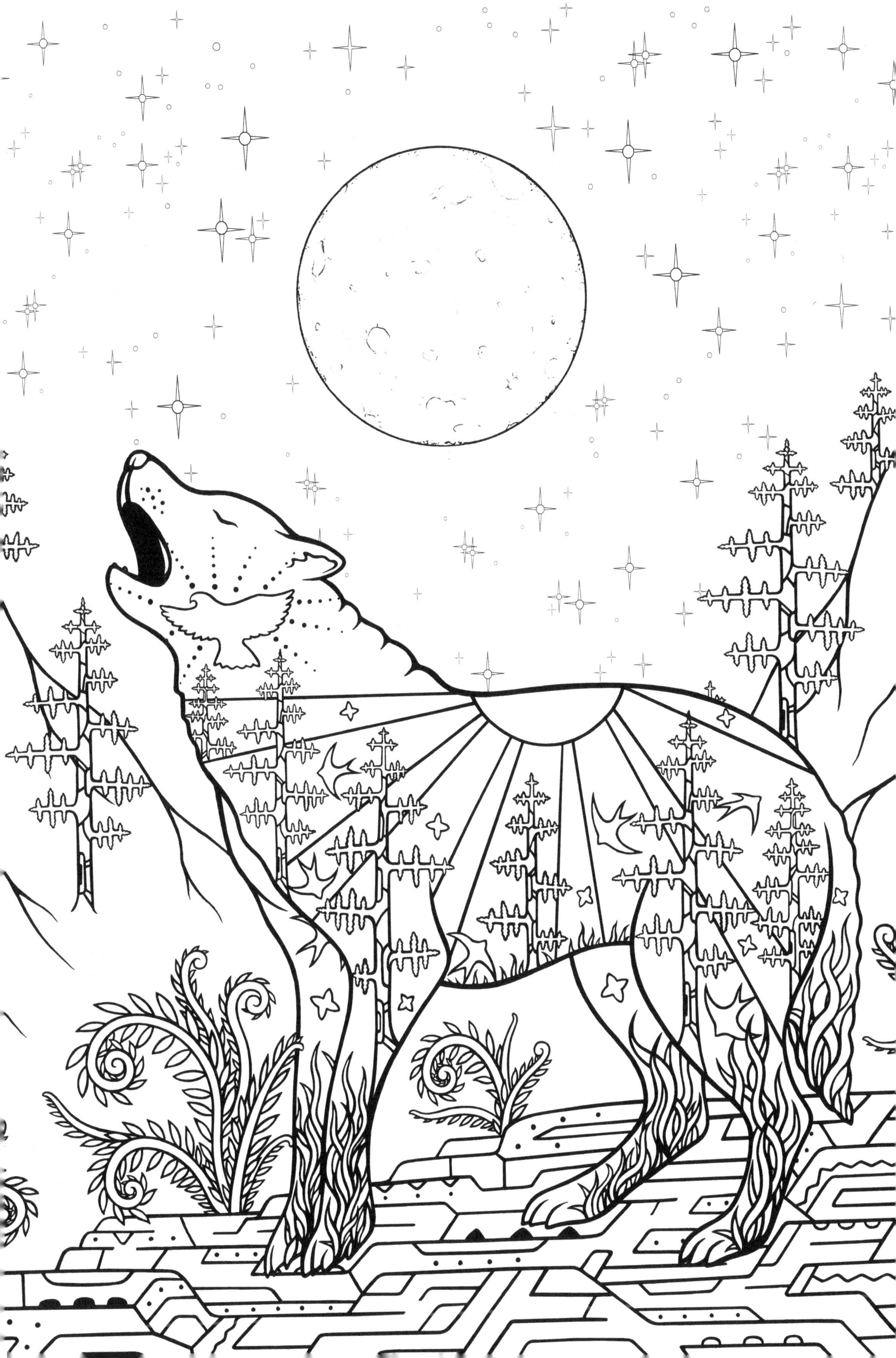

This panel highlights animals from the 3 realms of Earth = 'Mountain lion', Water = 'Salmon' and Air = 'Swift'. All three totems have some connection to adaptability, constant movement and change. Cats, fish and birds hold 3 distinct positions in the systems of totemic symbology, each holding significant value as power animals in their own right. The swift is the freer of the bunch with the ability to fly high and free, although can land and perch on the earth, and drink and sustain itself through water. The mountain lion is most at home with the earth element and poses some obstacles with the water and to a larger degree the 'air' element. The salmon is mostly confined to the water element, yet rests and feeds on the river bed ('earth'), yet also needs 'air' to survive. So this panel shows the interrelationship of these 3 totems in association with the principles of sustenance, sustainability and the very flux of the elements in the play of the life force.

Cats are usually lunar and feminine totems, however lions share a special association with solar energies and the balance between masculine and feminine power. The swift, being more gender-neutral, (A Mercurial totem) represents agility, adaptability, freedom of movement, and sets the scene for a more spring/summer, solarised, or lighthearted panel. The salmon represents here abundance, fertility and family happiness and carries a predominately feminine energy. The salmon totem relates to being unmoved by change and calamity and confers perpetual happiness, which is why it is sometimes associated with endlessness or eternal life. The salmon shows us how to attract abundance and draw more happiness into our life through the people or things that we cherish or love. It is connected here to enjoyment and fulfilment through the principles of sustenance, with the fuelling of fertility of our aspirations and dreams 'connected to' and nourished by the water element. In this particular cycle, 'water' manifests and nourishes 'earth' as physical or material forms.

Mountain lion's leadership stance has us facing the courage of self conviction to lead us where our heart finds true contentment, the balance of personal power and inner strength. This cat medicine can cause a tendency for us to always be vigilant or on guard. However, true self-empowerment in essence also demands us to be cautious at times, as to the motives of others to have control over, or influence our life direction, even in the subtlest or well-meaning of ways. Mountain lion energy is heavily associated with sound convictions and treading the path of self truth. The seven bird figures symbolise the awakening of light and greater life potential, with 7x3 = 21 (2+1 = 3). So '7' and '3' express the panel's main energetic syntax, relating largely to '3' for fertility, expansion and abundance. Each one of the 3 fish figures represent and elemental aspect of 'earth', 'water' and 'air'. Together these symbolises a generative or building force. The one solitary lion is a lioness and represents personal power, protective and guardian forces of the 'Goddess' or 'Cosmic Feminine' personified.

The connection with the cat totem and feminine power is well-known, yet here it relates specifically to the community, social sphere, family or pride. Those with mountain lion as one of their principle totems often find that things they put into motion are of great potential for world change, the community or world at large. This totem is strongly related to leadership, directorial positions and the Emperor/Empress figure, or King/Queen archetype. With this totem often comes lessons about true leadership, self sovereignty and self empowerment of the group, or greater whole. Often what serves our needs may need to go second in line at times to the needs of others, or sacrifice may be called upon in service of the greater plan or bigger picture. The good of the one is for the good of the group, however this can attract a certain degree of blaming or shaming from subordinates, those envious or jealous of the mountain lion's stance, authority, sense of self empowerment, position or presence.

The mountain figure conveys that 'like cats', sometimes we need to retreat to the solace of the cave to shelter ourself from the calamity and chaos of the outer world, to retrieve the subtle resounding echoes of self-truth. The real self-mastery reflected by this totem is that, at times, more gently assertive measures may be in order, where as at other times ferocity and showing your true colours and capabilities are clearly the order of the day. Like the responsibility of a King or Queen, mountain lion calls upon the spirit of self conviction to know the most appropriate path to tread, call into being, action or line of direction. When working with the mountain lion totem, colours that allow for vulnerability and refined sensitivity are useful at times, like pastel apricots, peach and pinks. These relate well also to the salmon and swift totems and in association with principles like aspiration, nurturance and fertility through nourishment. Variations of aqua, turquoise and blue complement these hues well and work well with the water elements. Likewise, yellow or saffron golds will also sweeten the mix, bringing further potential for abundance or growth. Otherwise, use colours that represent self empowerment to you, or that convey greater degrees of self-empowerment/self-conviction.

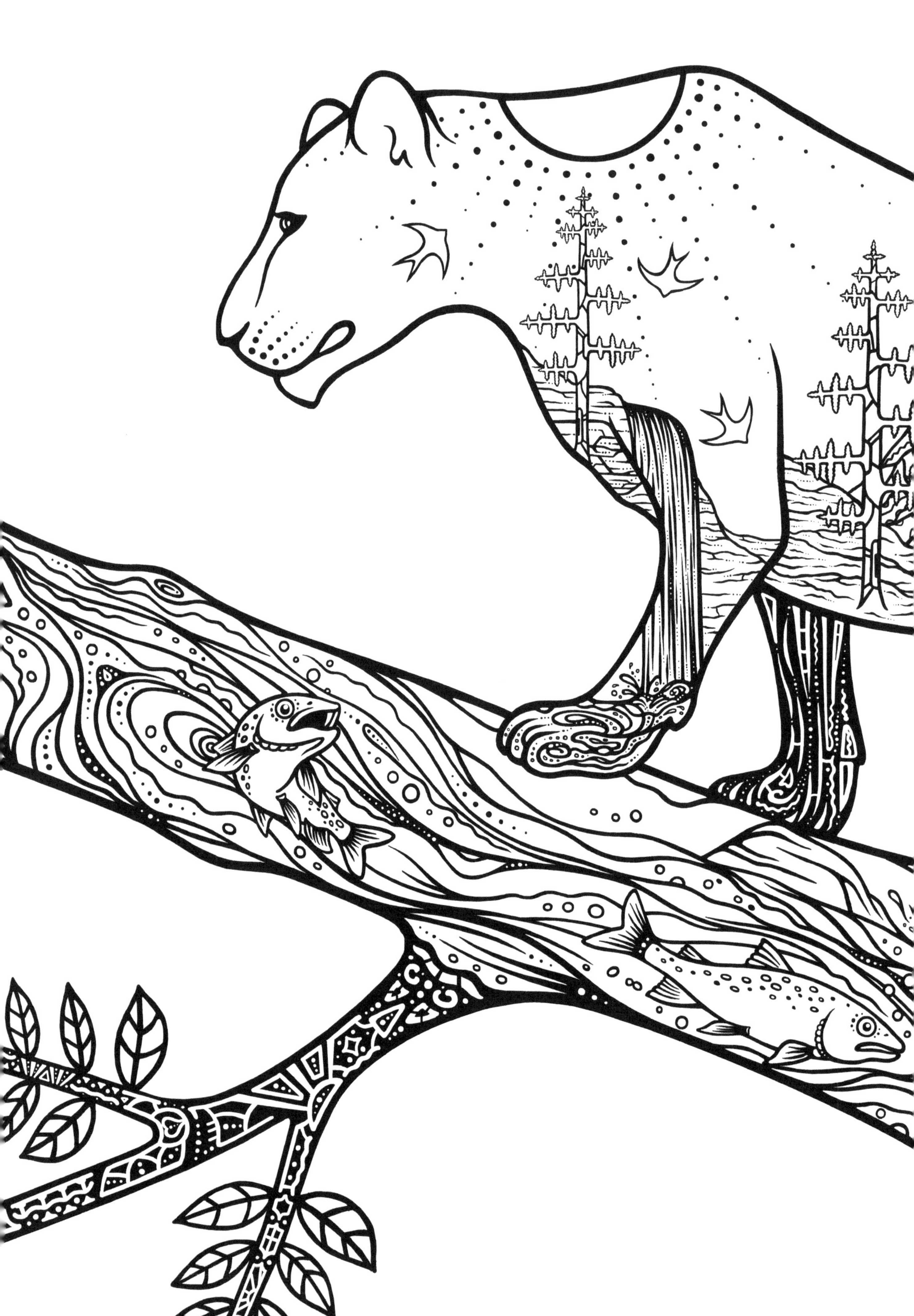

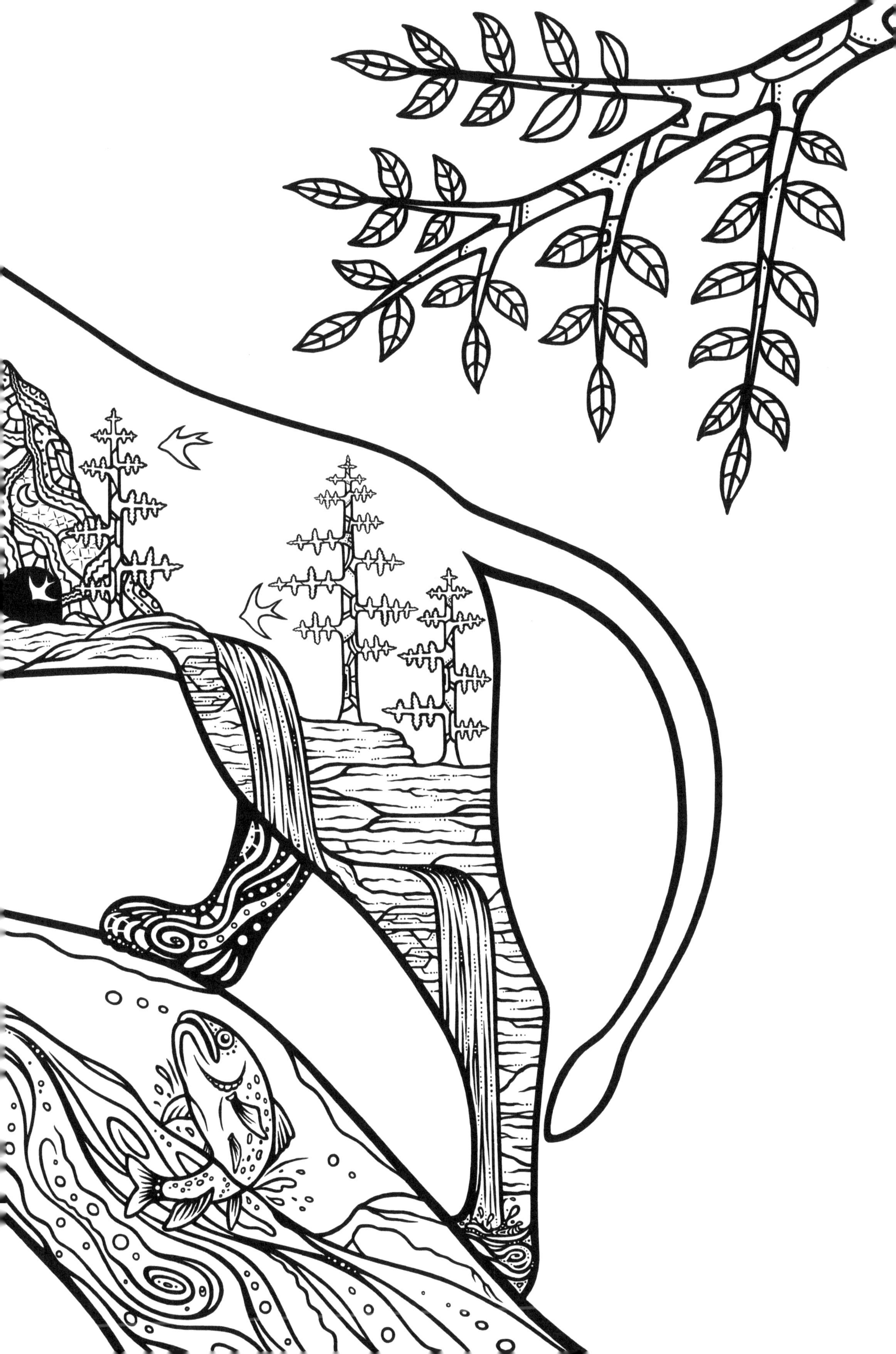

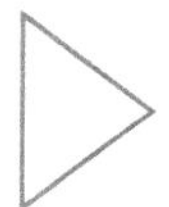

Bats are unique animals in that they are the only flying mammals on Earth. Symbols of rebirth, they are lunar totems who are seldom seen in the day, which reinforces their association with darkness and the very 'Cave of Creativity', the 'Womb state' or 'Inner Earth'. In Ancient China they were associated with 'happiness' and 'longevity' and in the Cultural Traditions of South America they are associated with 'initiation' and 'rebirth'. As lunar totems they relate somewhat to other 'birthing' and 'earthing' totems like the 'whale' and 'snake'. They also interrelate with totems like 'black cats', 'ravens' and the 'bear' in association with the subconscious state, 'the cave within', mystery and magic. Butterflies also represent a somewhat lighter equivalent and 'solar' version if you will, of the bat, that is more aligned with transformation into a totally free and renewed state of being. Bats are more associated with a specific area of 'transmutation', relating more to the physical or 'Earth' element (Butterflies are more representative of 'Air' and 'Fire').

Bat energies remind us that at times we need to remove the old to allow for the new – whether it be ingrained habits or stubborn mental patterns, emotional hurdles, physical obstacles, or some other element of our life that is not flowing smoothly. The bat kind of renewal can at times be difficult or abrupt, associated with astrological forces like Pluto, Saturn, Ketu or Chiron. Life's difficulties often come at junctures, and when bat energy presents itself, difficult subjects or aspects of our life may need to be acknowledged or dealt with in a way that is best for the long haul, and not just a superficial quick fix. In 2020 Pluto will be involved in initiating great change on the planet, with a rebirth of its own taking place for our world at large. It is more like the catalyst for the change or transmutation to occur and it has been hundreds of years since similar transits of such significance for 'World Change'. A new way of utilising resources at our disposal may indeed be in order and a birthing of new perspective or outlook for Earth, or the way we initiate action moving forward.

The symbology here is a mix of baby bats and butterflies to soften the otherwise deeper or intense 'otherwise-known' aspects of the bat totem that we find in legends and folklore. Bats often get a bad rap for this reason and are one of the most misunderstood totems, which draws some aversion to what would otherwise be a natural part of life junctures associated with healthy transformation and renewal. They are a totem that has great power encased in what lies beyond the flip side of fear. If we dare to do something great, something monumental, or that will have great change for the better, then a certain shift or transmutation of certain elements often needs to occur – be re-ordered, transmuted, or re-shaped in alignment with the utilitarian purpose of the new reality. For If we fail to acknowledge the necessity or specific need for future change, then we are prone to averting or resisting the natural flow of life forces associated with transformation and associated necessary action.

So the bat is an animal of transition and shares that some transitions are unavoidable. It represents the coming out of darkness, ignorance and fear – and in the case of the bat totem, suggests the best medicine at times may actually be the absence of fear in the face of the inevitable. The inevitability of change, of newness and letting go of the old and empowering yourself to truely create the vision of self renewal that suits your current life juncture. Colours for the bat/butterfly mandala may be anything that is warm and earthy. However, you can mix in pinks and violets for gentle transformation and newfound aspiration. Avoid black to keep from the artwork/process becoming too dark or heavy, yet maybe use accents of dark chocolate browns, rusty browns for effect, even deep green. Lighter mid tan and beige tones can also help lighten up the image and provide openness. Alternatively, mix in some earthy or even warm green hues for a contrasting effect. Golden yellow and saffron hues and even pastel orange can work well for the solar, upper aspect of the image. So there is great potential for variation in this mandala and the colours chosen depends directly on the degree of transformation, transmutation, self renewal or renewed aspiration that you so choose.

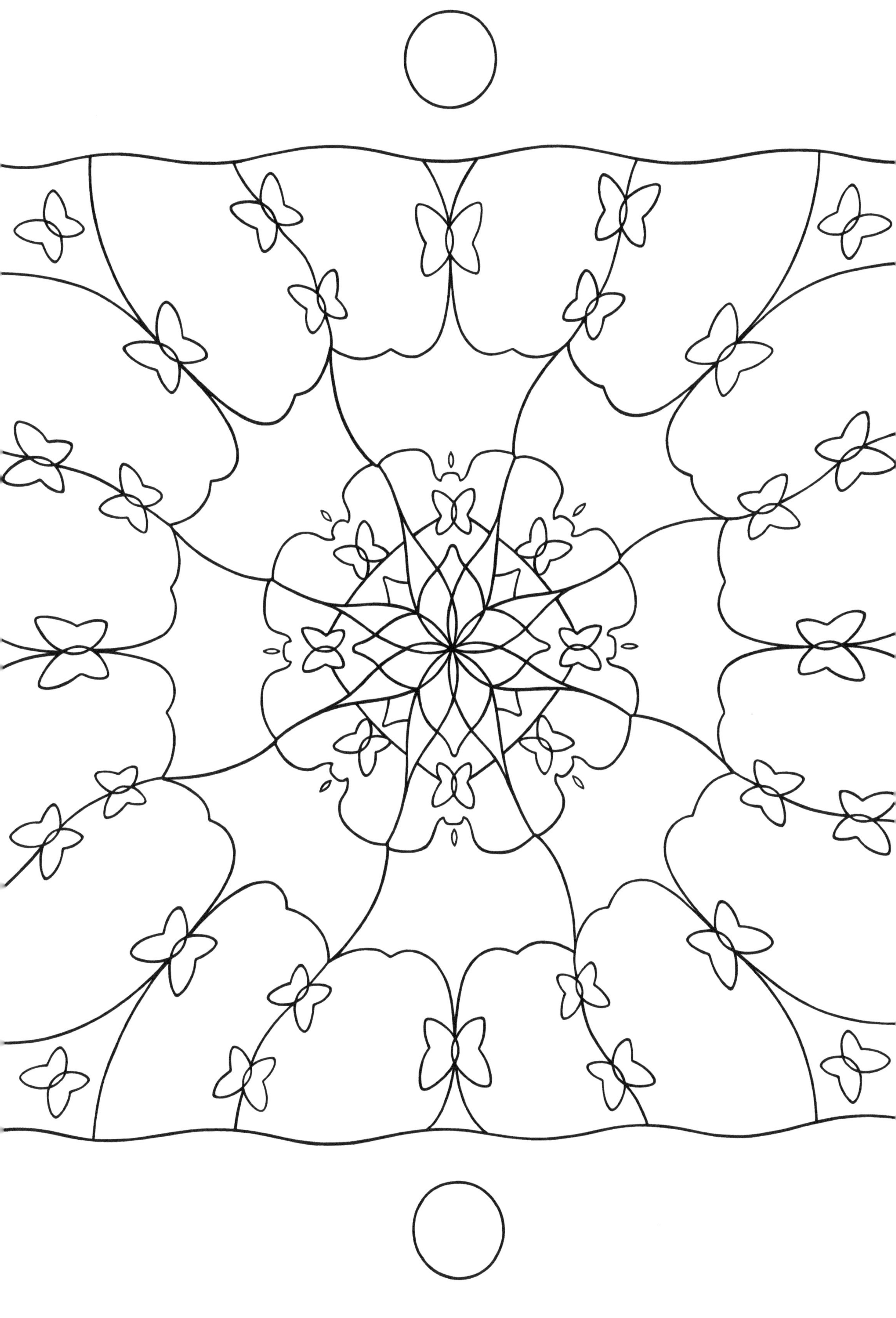

This panel is stylised utilising tribal or tattoo styled glyphs. It depicts the multidimensional interrelationship between the 'Inner Earth' and 'Open Air' worlds in association with the celestial cycles of time. The above/below beholds a balance of masculine and feminine dynamics. This is evidenced here by the central 15 ellipse figures resting half above and half below the horizon, which symbolise the fullness of material creation and the 15 days of the lunar month in Jyotish (Traditional Indian Astrology). Then there are '12' flanked mound sections supporting the hawk and solar orb and '12' energy waves trailing the wings of the bat below - a number associated with universal integrity. The 13th element here, being the middle dimensional doorway that connects the 2 solar and lunar realms. This shares graphically how the mystical number 13 is closely interrelated with the number 12, with dimensional doorways that relate to new octaves of expansion or growth, as we see in the music scale, or lunar seasons and cycles. There are creation voids (13th element) that exist between the 12 note sets of octaves of creative expression. The '24' 'solar/lunar' unison represents here the 24 hours of the solar day/night cycle. If we add the 12 elements of Solar orb + 1 Sun and 12 elements of Lunar orb + 1 Moon - we get a 'double 13', for the combined total solar/lunar day of 26, a number associated with the fulfilment of aspirations, contentment and the higher octave of personal karma or self growth.

The jaguar represents impeccability, integrity and the balance of power connected with right action. The jaguar's impeccable traits are related to its abidance to cosmic law. If it sees something to be true and right its sticks to it with a sense of duty or honour. The jaguar is a popular totem throughout ancient and modern South and North American cultures. It is a powerful totem in Indigenous Cosmology and Dreamtime legends, related to the adherence to the laws of nature and the interrelationship between feminine or lunar cycles and the celestial rhythms of time. Related totemically to the leopard, both species are in the 'panther' genus. Like all panther species, which have a intimate connection to vibrations and the subtlety of sound, the jaguar has a strong lunar sensitivity. Here we see the jaguar absorbing or attuning to the energies of the Moon, symbolising this totem's role or key association with feminine rights of passage and ceremony related to the 'Cosmic Feminine' and the 'Lunar Realms'.

The bat totem is often misunderstood in its association with rebirth, transmutation and change from one life juncture or space to another. Relating to the earth and fire elements, bats carry a somewhat deep or heavier totemic load, where as butterflies are much lighter totems for transformation, relating to inspiration of 'fire' and the freedom and adaptability of 'air'. The bat unearths awareness surrounding the shadows of the self, felt at times as pain and intensity in the body (our earth frame), through which we come to experience or know our sense of humanity, our interconnectedness. It often relates to some kind of death or demise, necessary release, or letting go. When something dies, the memory impressions and experiences it/they shared live on to influence others. Even the physical remains by nature goes on to nurture growth, providing nourishments for other life forms in the ecosystem. So in embracing death we are experiencing life in its continuum of cyclic growth and renewal. This is the combined syntax of the jaguar and bat totems, and their association with sensitivity or receptivity to Earth's cycles of Nature and our integration with them through cycles of time.

The top half of the image may work better with more boldly contrasting hues, like violet, magenta, orange or gold for the sun and rays, with indigo, purple or indigo (or brown) accent hues for the hawk. Otherwise, experiment with various shading and contrasting hues of your choice, as shading and toning itself gives greater access to the subtlety of energy and vibration. For the bat try chocolate, shaded with tan, burgundy, accented with complementary colours like pink and aqua, or even saffron or gold highlights. Try colours that depict deeper, darker or more earthy qualities towards the bottom, with lighter, freer or more airy on the top.

The hawk symbolises sharpness of perception, wisdom and truth. It represents potential sacredness that comes through increased awareness and intuitive insight. As the 'Forest Dreaming' volume is dedicated to a predominance of bird life, the hawk totem here represents the summit of potential similar to the 'Eagle' or 'Whale' totems. These totems are often used to symbolise an element of supremacy, higher knowing, or to represent expanded awareness or higher dimensions of growth. Hawks and Eagles are solar totems, as we see in the Egyptian, Native American and Indian Traditions. Here it connects the inner earth and feminine of below with the outer and radiant light of the Sun (masculine) above. The hawk also has a special connection to messages and communications form higher, subtler, or more refined dimensions of reality (aqua/electric blue), or inner intuitive knowing (indigo).

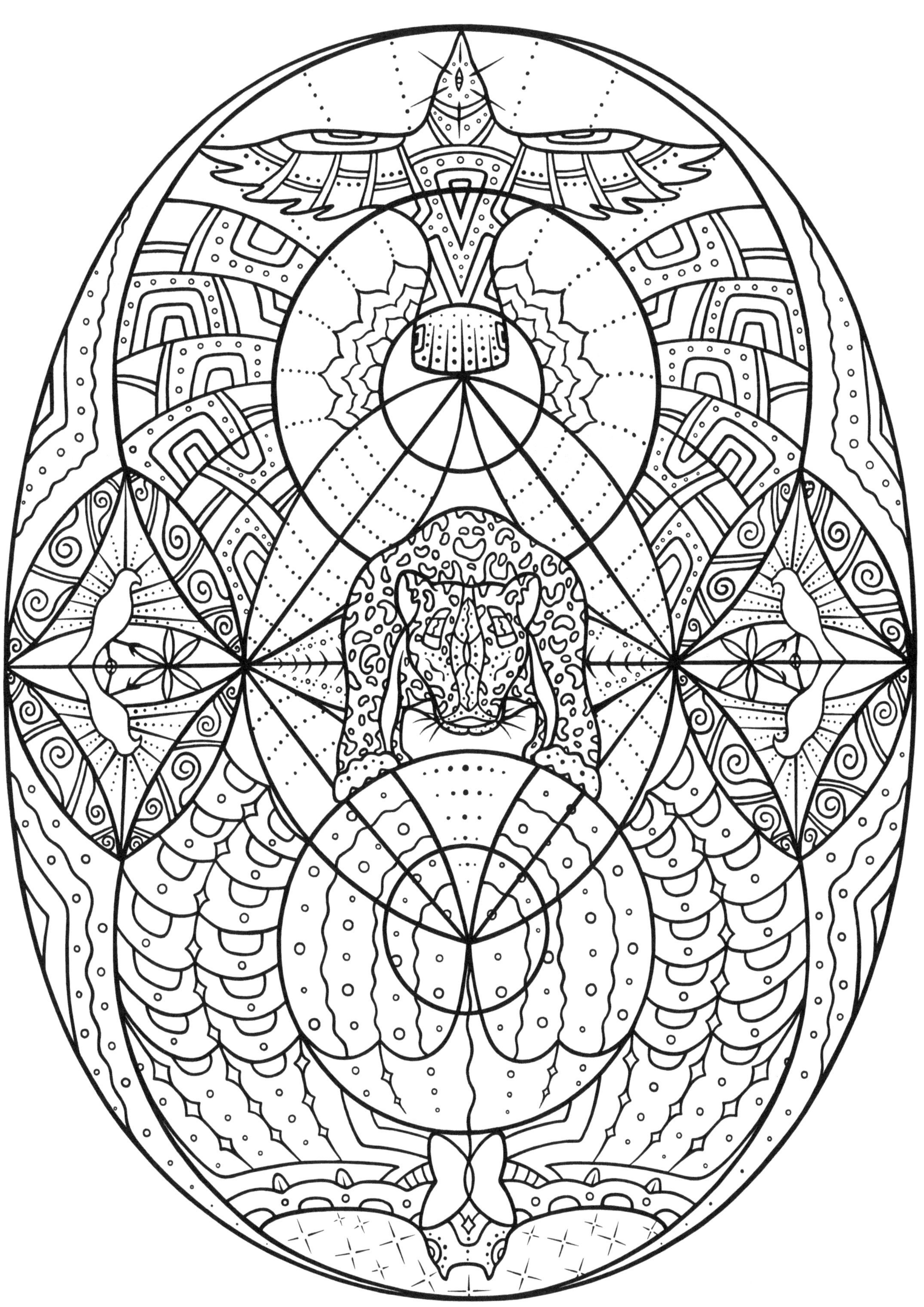

This panel shares an open enchanted woodland scene, complete with the deer's secluded private lagoon. Alive with forest ferns, flowers, crystals, critters, toadstools and aquatic plants. The setting is the Winter/Spring juncture, where new life springs into form and the forest comes alive with vibrancy and wonder. The forest deer is an enigmatic and gentle totem with lunar association and in Traditional Indian Astrology, as the Moon rides on a celestial deer. We also see deer held sacred in association with 'sensitivity to energy', 'mystery' and 'magic' in many legends and folklore. The deer represents the special magic of innocence that lures us into a relationship of mystery, or with the unknown. There is a special connection to imagination and to the celestial currents of energy, similar to its brother 'elk' totem. However, deer is more of an inner celestial connection to energetic currents, seasons and cycles. The elk totem is a symbol of cosmic energy and associated more with the grounding of celestial forces, with the deer being more connected to the attunement and inner impact of such forces or energies in our environment, and in our mental or emotional world.

Deer is connected very much here to the sacredness of the Moon cycle, to Moon folklore and ceremony, which works with celestial and seasonal rhythms. Deer energy shares with us that the Moon cycle represents the abundance of Nature and that there are defined points in the ebb and flow of this cycle where the awakening of energy happens. It is a sensitivity to innocence and newness like that of a baby or new birth. It shares the need to be gentle with ourself and environment at hand, or the impact on family/community. Deer relates directly to having a refined sensitivity to sight and sound, to reading or sensing the subtle vibrations and impulse of Nature, and the more magical, or unseen worlds. The wood swallows can often be seen gliding or darting in strange flight patterns that are very geometric and synchronised. They actually use a kind of sound navigation and signalling involved in their inter-communion of flight aerobatics or flight display, which is one aspect of this panel's connection to sound waves, or the soundscape that a bustling forest glen reverberates or resounds. They represent here the welcome spirit and call of sound through song and harmony, acted out through both their calls and their dynamic and lively synchronised flight patterns.

The deer, squirrel and rabbit each have a connection to sensitivity and the spirit of sisterhood. The oak trees are in new growth as are the fern fronds and early spring blooms. This panel lends itself to a wide variety of colouring options. One way to make the artwork impactful is to make the sun somewhat the central focus, as without it, the image would lose some of its appeal. Shading with various softer tones in the sky can work well with gold and yellow shades for the sun itself. All manner of hues can be shaded into the forest flowers, mushrooms and tree glyphs, with this panel being one of the most exploratory in nature. The squirrel has some connection to play and kinship through sisterhood (largely feminine panel), to joy and curiosity. The rabbit is a totem associated with deep sensitivity and the flip side of dread or fear, which oversensitivity can exacerbate or create. The deer is also associated with sensitivity, yet more in line with how her brotherly 'elk' totem relates to the sensitivity to celestial currents and energetic assimilation that pours into the forest world. With these traits in mind, soft pastel colours would work well into the syntax and overall colour symmetry of the design.

The deer totem itself relates to soft pastel emanations as seen in the 'light of the Moon', which as we know in nature can be anywhere from soft pastel orange through to a rare soft 'pastel blue'. Many colours may suit as it's a very lively and active panel. See the Squirrel panel in Masterclass 4 for further colouring options and Masterclass 10 at the back of the book for colours relative to other forest animals or elements. Also, it will help the panel to include a variety green and brown tones, Whether it be green-brown, tan, beige, caramel or deep chocolate brown hues. These will provide important colour relief in the artwork and save from it becoming too 'colour busy'.

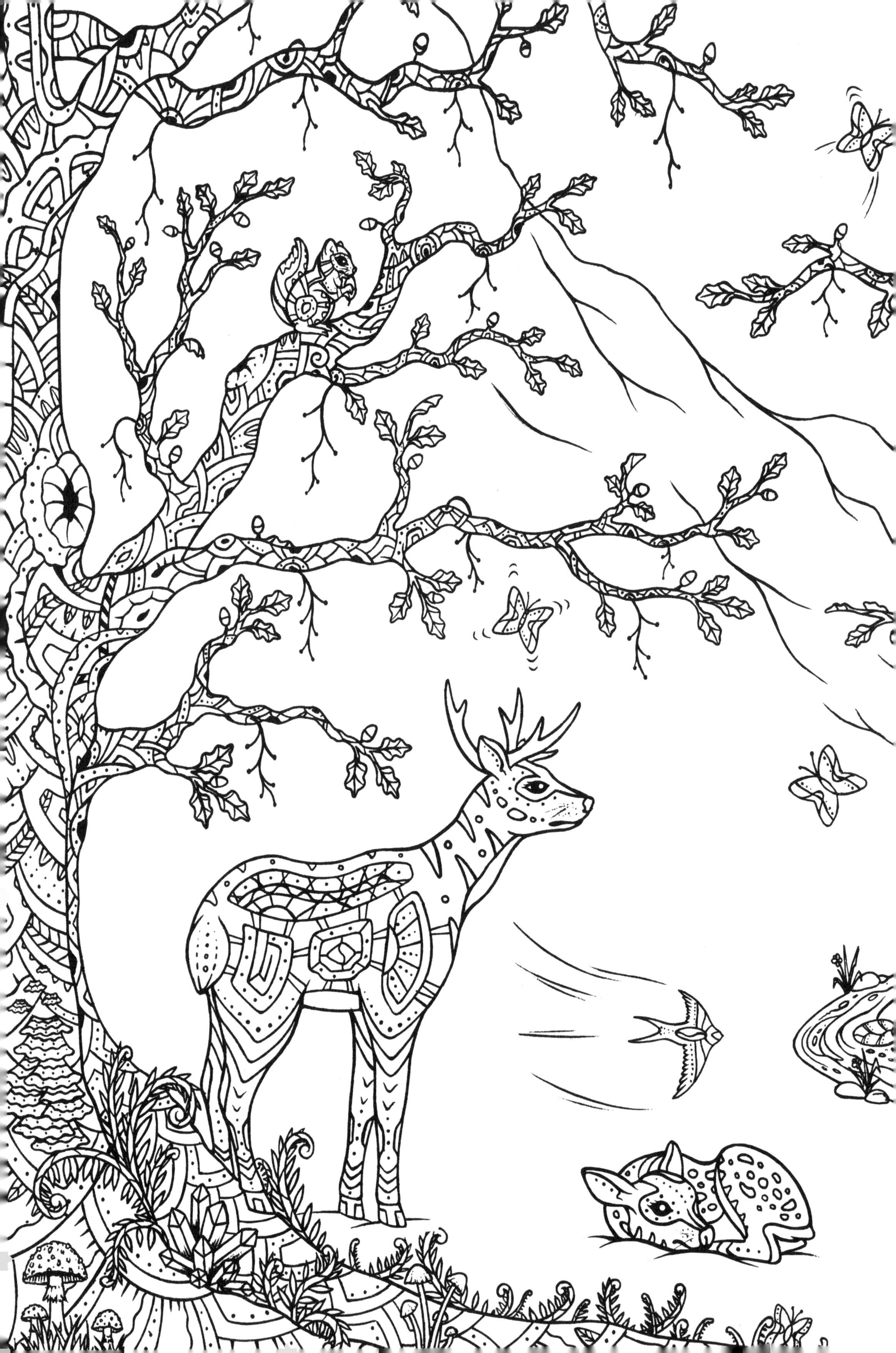

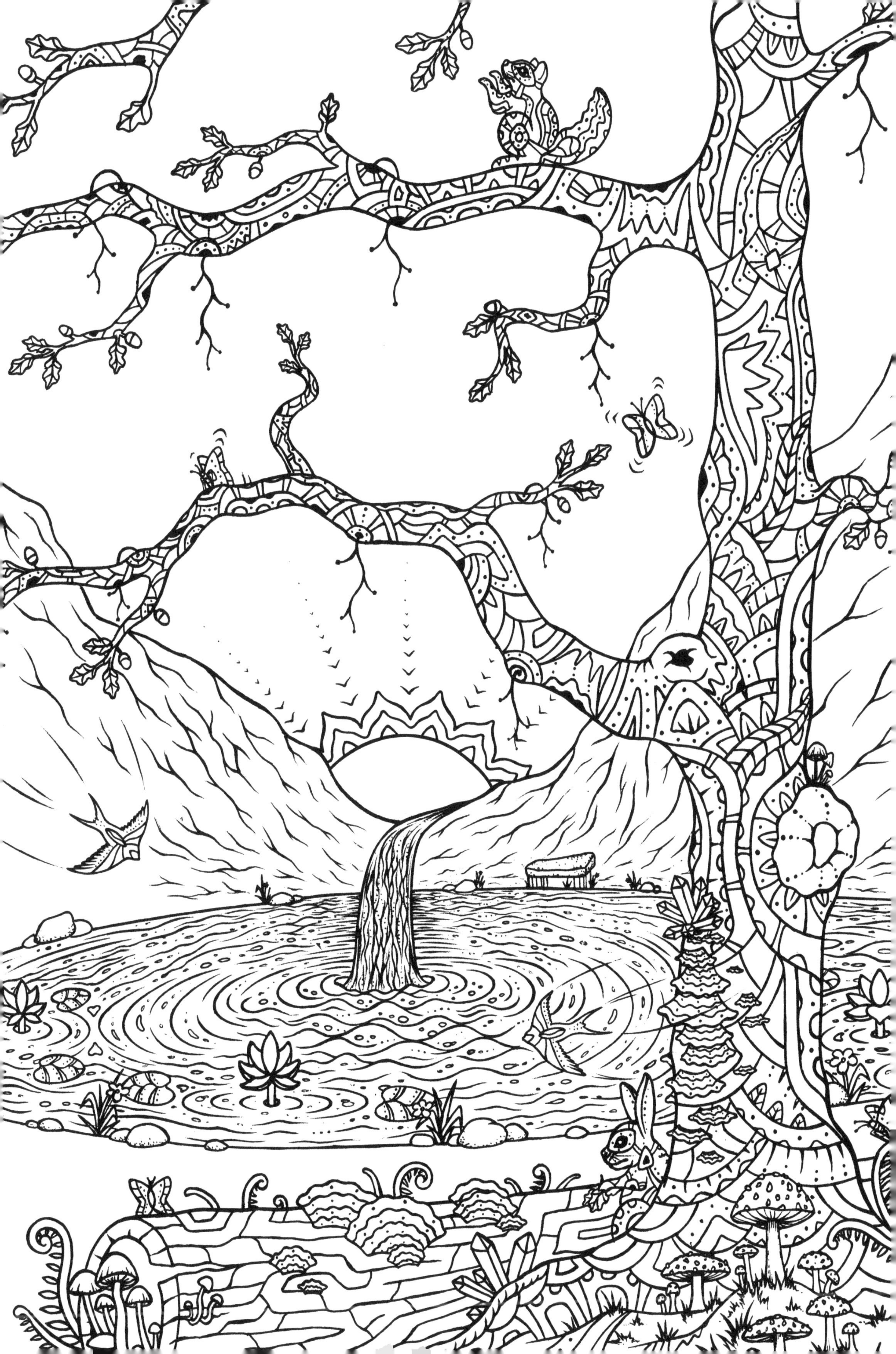

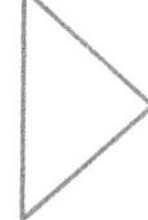

This panel is inspired by years of working with various species of songbirds in the photographic arena in the wild. Songbirds are associated with the freedom of expression of sound, to the principle of play and sharing the uniqueness of sound expression. Some of the birds in the forest seem to possess highly cryptic sound knowledge, by where their call is encapsulating something profound and deep. Others express a more simplistic mating call that is very transparent and self-evident. It can be helpful to feel the colourful expression of the sounds of the songbird as you colour, or maybe even listen to music with bird sounds in it to access even deeper the world of these melodious forest birds. As colours are light frequencies of sound on a subtle level, a greater degree of intricacy was woven into the panel design. This allows for some interesting colour combinations. You could choose to reference some forrest songbirds from nature like the robin family, the whistler or wren. Even referencing parrot colours would work well for this design. Birds often have different colours for the male and female in nature, so this could also be factored into your colouring choices, maybe with a pair that complement each other. This panel lends itself to both solid colouring and more subtle colour shading.

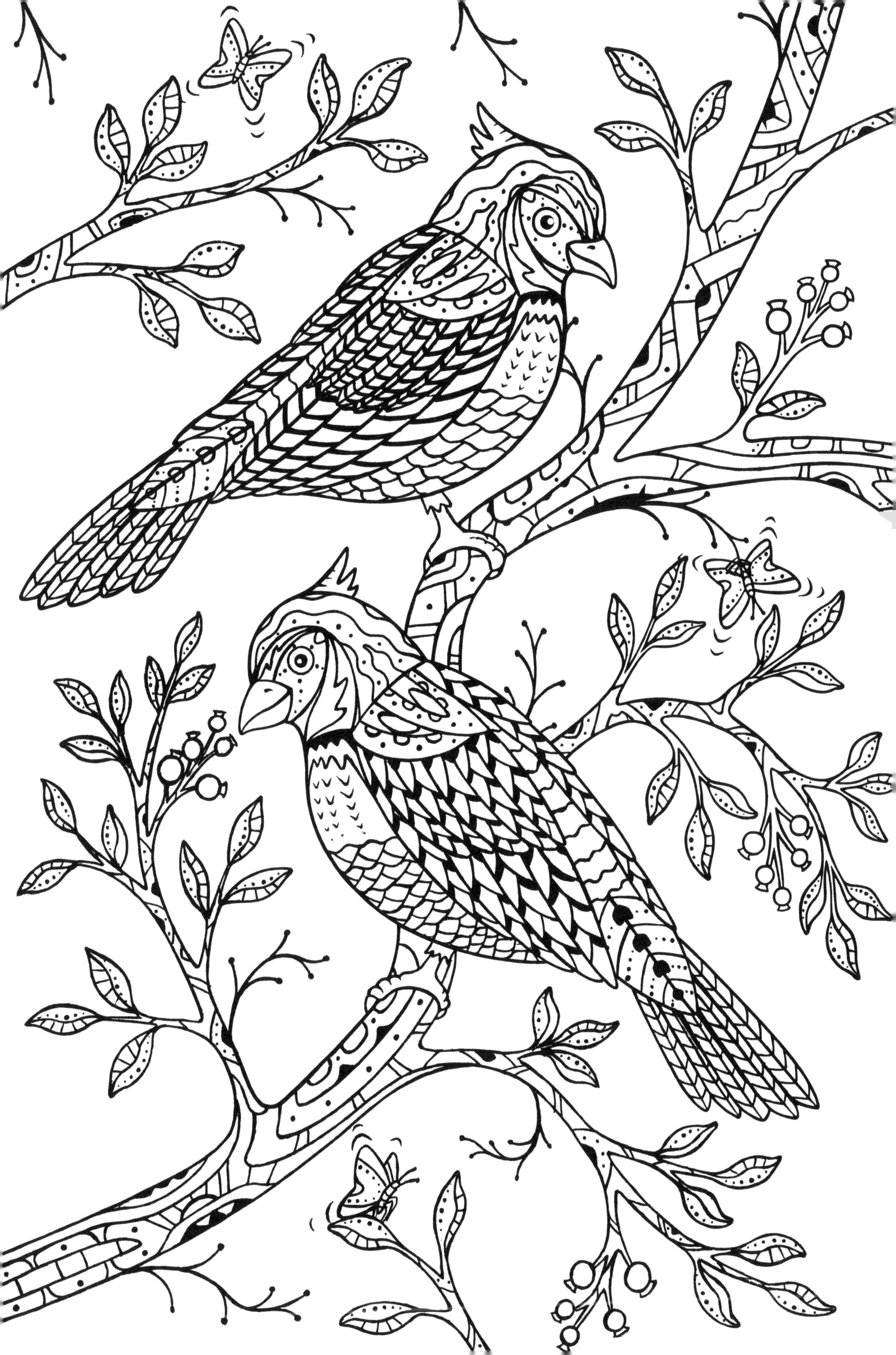

This is one of the most activating and enlivening mandalas – moving into the year 2020, a time when these energies are indeed welcomed by our beloved home 'Earth'. It shares that we need to lighten the load, help relieve the burdensome nature of those with heavy hearts and offer trust in Earth's transformation that is in play. The central core energy of this mandala reminds us we are all part of the change and renewal. The symbolism of this mandala is direct in what it conveys. Its central core qualities are harmony, tranquility and balance. It does not convey passive energetics though, as to achieve necessary harmony on Earth requires effort, right action and the wise use and balance of resources and wealth at our disposal. The mandala has a combination of archetypal shapes, symbols and animal totems, many of which speak directly to our conscious and subconscious mind. No colour guidance is given here, as this nature mandala is open to a wide variety of possibilities. It is your unique signature opportunity to share your view of world change, world colour-harmony, or whatever you see fit to bring to the table and co-communicate with Mother Earth 'Our Home'.

Utilising bird graphics and symbology is a great way to move energy in artwork and imagery, with diverse varieties often representing or depicting specific qualities or characteristics. Swifts and swallows are often related through mythology and folklore and have come to share similar symbolic meaning for this reason. Also, the fact that they often represent the positive, welcome energies of the spring, hope, home and new beginnings. Traditions have them associated with being welcomed home, loyalty/disloyalty of spirit and dynamics surrounding wavering or enduring love. Their totemic qualities and body shape symbolism helps discern between the two. The swift for instance is associated with agility, assertiveness and change that brings auspiciousness to future events in time. The swallow carries some of these qualities, yet also relates also to the security, protection and warmth of the domestic or home environment. The two birds are in different sub-orders, with swifts actually being in the hummingbird family, whereas swallows are passerines. Swifts interrelate with the wren and hummingbird totems, while the swallow interrelates with other passerines totems like robins and parrots, in associated with qualities like domestic happiness, feathering the nest, intimacy and the need for affection and love. This mandala incorporates these combined dynamics, associated with enlivening and securing harmony and happiness on Earth and into the Environment.

The central branched trunks represent reaching out to current world and environmental concerns that keep Mother Earth happy and sustainable for generations to come. Grounded and planted firmly in the awareness of Earth's needs is the basis for happiness to be allowed or shared together as a civilisation. The butterfly figures symbolise the transformation in place, as we are at a sensitive juncture at this point in time with Nature's Eco Systems and growing Environmental Concerns – yet this mandala radiates 'Hope' and 'Auspiciousness'. It is pulsating and alive with fertility and potential. The swifts represent ever-new potential, agility and change, with the flower and heart shaped figures symbolising compassion and kindness, through which we find sensitivity, cohesiveness and the reason to care. The serpentine borders in the outer perimeter represent the the 12 divisions of time associated with with the solar day and the cosmic energy personified as the Goddess 'Shakti'. They have here an 'Earth Snake' energy, consistent with Chinese Astrology. The 6 solar orbs represent the 6 feminine-polarity zodiac signs of Taurus, Cancer, Virgo, Scorpio, Capricorn and Pisces. A great deal of celestial receptivity comes to Earth through these signs, especially in current times, allowing for openness to change and better solutions to world and environmental needs/concerns. Colour freely, as this panel is one that may benefit from colouring multiple times or photocopying and trying different colour combinations, as qualities like 'Freedom' and 'Unity in Diversity' are core quality of this design.

Specific meaning and symbolism is given in this book relative to each design or panel, with there being a few bird panels in the 'Forrest Dreaming' book to cover the importance and significance that they each share. Also, they are often totems associated with Spring, Happiness, Freedom, Contentment and Joy, themes or qualities that this volume focuses on.

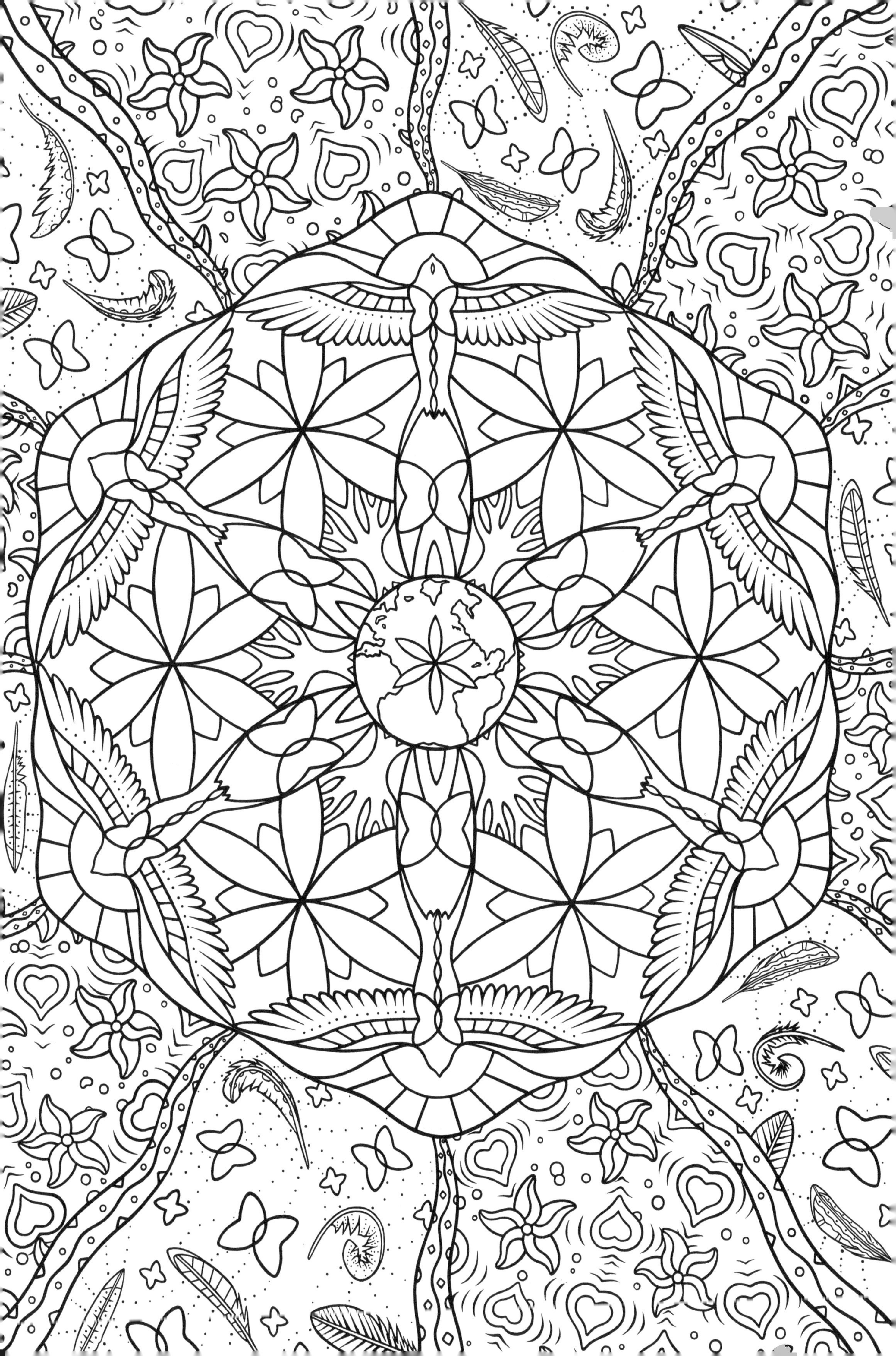

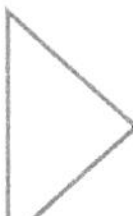

This two-page panel was conceptualised whilst watching fascinating documentary Nature footage of Madagascar. Madagascar is unique like Australia, in that many rare animal species still exist related to the native landmass of 'Gondwana', said to have existed over 500 million years ago. Animals in Australia and Madagascar are found nowhere else on Earth and this is a key fascination with the magic and wonder of the native fauna and flora of these great lands. The totemic qualities here are diverse, with specific totems like the bat, butterfly, chameleon and kingfisher. The totems here offer a balance of masculine and feminine dynamics, with the birds representing the solar or masculine dynamics along with the tree body. The chameleon represents androgyny and is considered a 'gender-neutral' totem associated with adaptability and change. Otherwise, the panel is designed to get lost for hours in the energies of the Madagascan woodland. Colours could be entirely of your choice with most elements, although some well placed aqua and rich royal blues would suit the kingfisher. Kingfishers come in many colours, so it is often good to source colour options from the internet. The flowers and butterflies would suit many colour combinations too. One approach if this panel seems overwhelming at first is too pick some tan hues with maybe neutral chocolate browns (browns that are not quite red-brown or green-brown) and add these first as a bulk of the tree sections. This way you can then build up other colours and accent the stylised patterns and glyphs on the tree branches to suit.

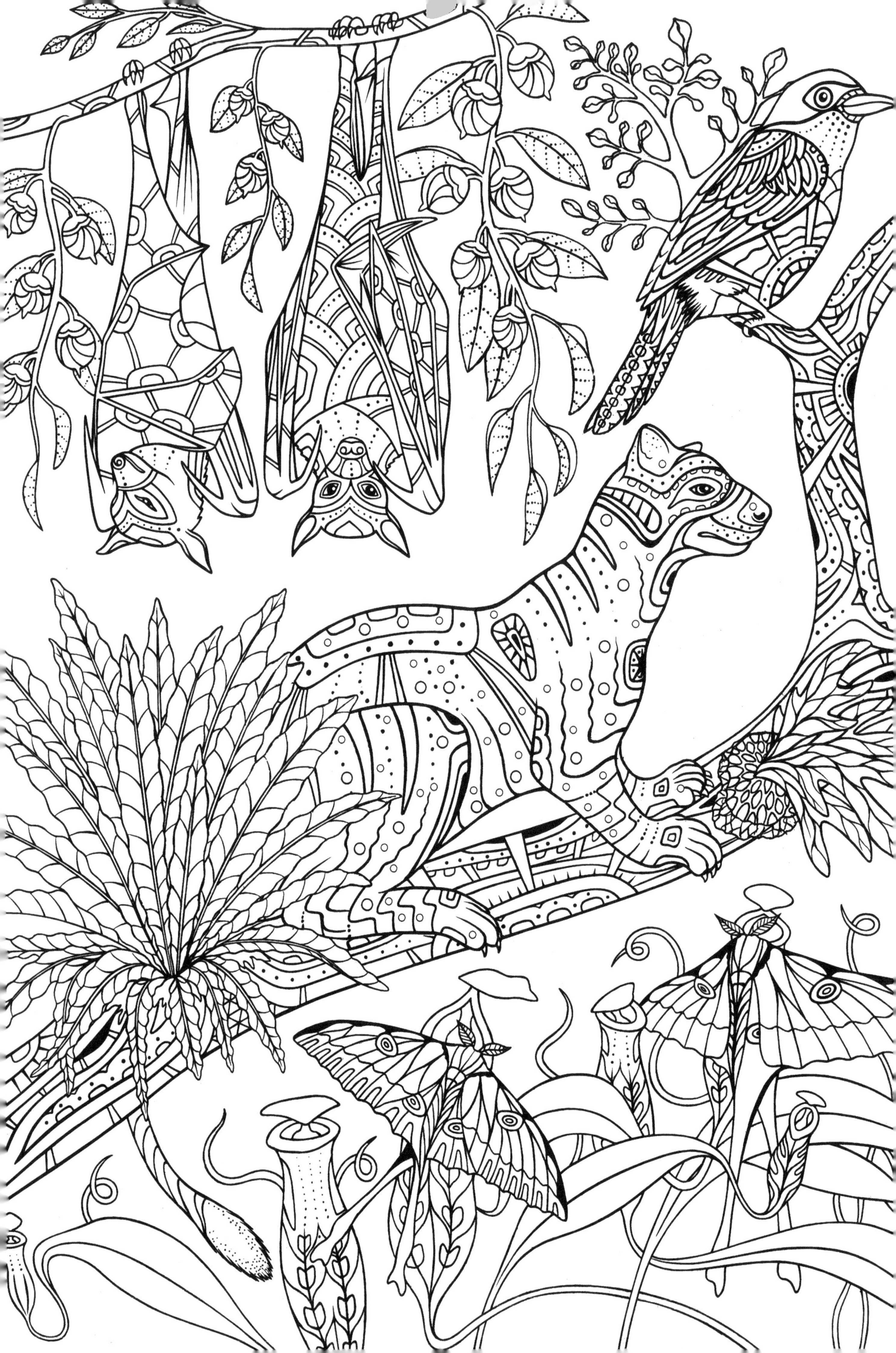

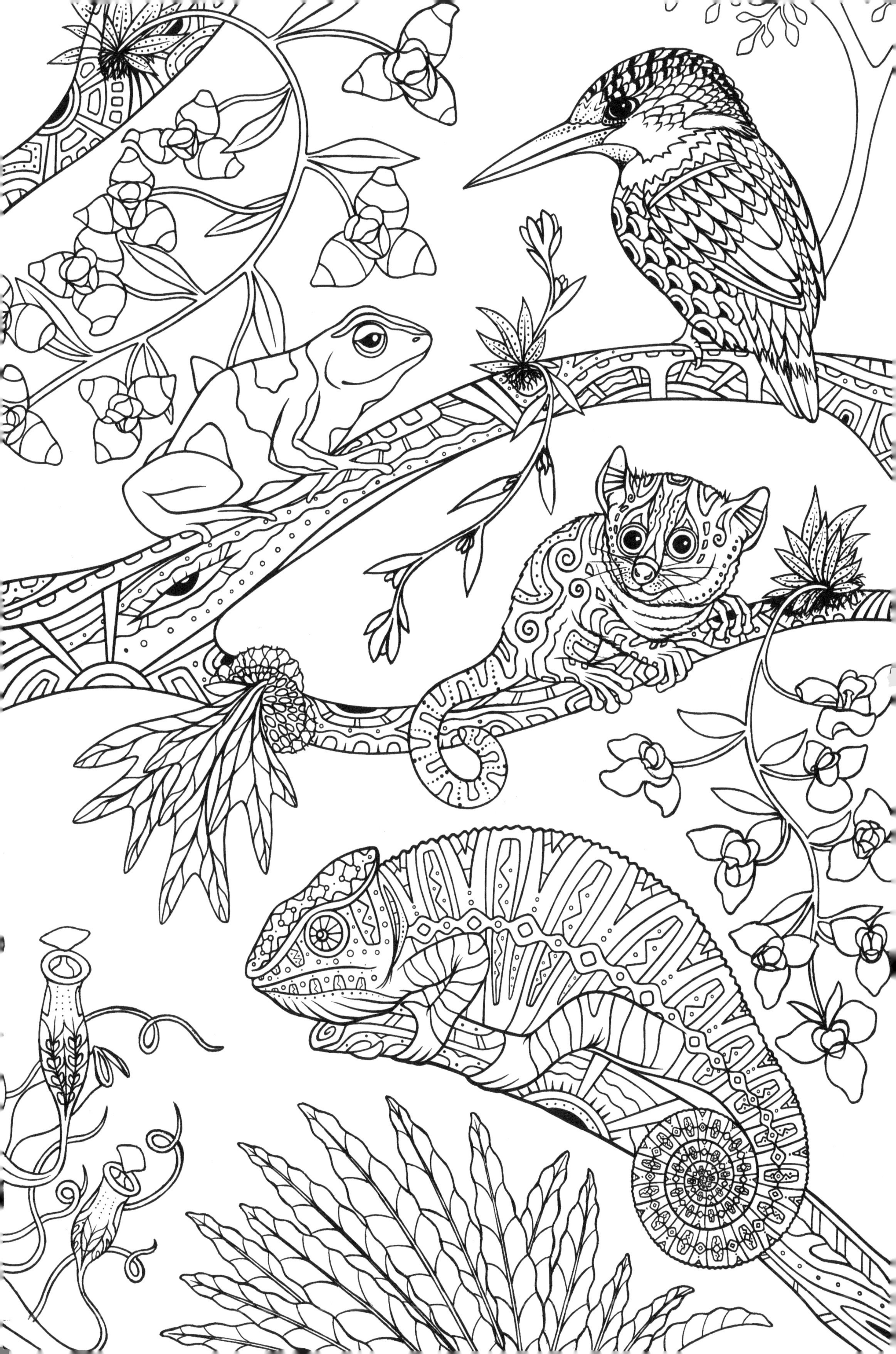

This panel is alive with the call of the forest wren, who brings the vibrant and soulful message of song. The wren totem represents boldness and resourcefulness and is associated with bringing messages and wisdom through from other dimensions. It is an adventurous, gregarious and high velocity totem, keen to share and express through sonic melody and sacred sound. Wrens, as with many songbirds, relate to Saraswati, who beyond her religious association is a Universal Goddess of 'Wisdom' and 'Music'. The wren totem holds great potential for conveying knowledge through sacred sound, along with sharing, teaching or general learning through the medium of sound. We know this with most songbirds, which display beautiful melodies, with some even singing together in harmonies, or in a call-and-response manner. However, do we ever think of the knowledge aspect or impact imparted through song and the sacredness of sound? With the wren totem, to sing is to share, and to share is to teach or impart knowledge in some regard. Wrens are even known to impart signature sound learnings to their chicks whilst they are still in their eggs, which the chicks use as a signature sound phrase for communication with their mother once they hatch.

Some sources associate the wren totem with Infidelity and disloyalty, however this is often a superficial and often misunderstood aspect of the totem, which relates to yearly or seasonal fertility junctures of the bird, and 'non-human' kingdom. The fairy wren sings in the face of enmity and struggle. As a totem, it suggests energising or meeting that which serves negative ends with upliftment and joy, similar to the hummingbird totem. The world needs these totems at present as there is a tendency to get caught up in shading and shaming, or calamity associated with the darker side of materialism, self-obsession, possessiveness and a constant need for competition, comparison or self validation. Sharing in the uniqueness of joy through song has the potential for shaping the new future dimensions of growth for the 'Earth to come', which is part of the message and impact these inspiring songbird totems have to share. For when we share our uniqueness without the need to compete, just purely to impart creative expression, where is there room for measuring up, or the limitations of needless self-perpetuated validation?

The wren calls because it is joyous and has something to share and calls to the spur of the moment and speaks of the raw un-orchestrated power of sound. The wren totem shares that there is always a new melody just waiting to resound through the forest. Its energies work on healing the environment, community and sibling rivalries, along with providing positive and uplifting vibrations to co-communal ventures and the society in general. It is not an idol totem and brings much fascination, new perspective and boundless creative vigour. It is an energy that generates abundance, yet often with little care for owning or capitalising on the abundance or wealth generated. It is more about the generous generation or expression of wealth, creative energy, or creative capacity that relates to our true sense of self value. In this sense, it signifies and abundance of creative potential or creative knowing. To ground the high velocity of the wren, we have here the forest brook, or spring, accompanied with the energies of the salmon totem. The salmon in folklore represents abundance, perpetual or self-generated fertility, being unmoved by change and the obstacles of life. The salmon shares how to attract abundance and draw into our life the things we enjoy, or through which we will find greater fulfilment together.

Colours for this panel can be lively and activating in general. Colours that symbolise abundance and growth like bold yellows and warm greens will work well with many aspects of the image, or as contrasting accent hues. For the wrens, maybe look to images on the internet for fairy wren plumage, as they come in a wide variety of hues and colour combinations. Also, see the colour version of panel 1 (*Left side) in Masterclass 7 for a full breakdown on colour distribution and further 'colour-musing' or enlivening 'colour contemplation' tips.

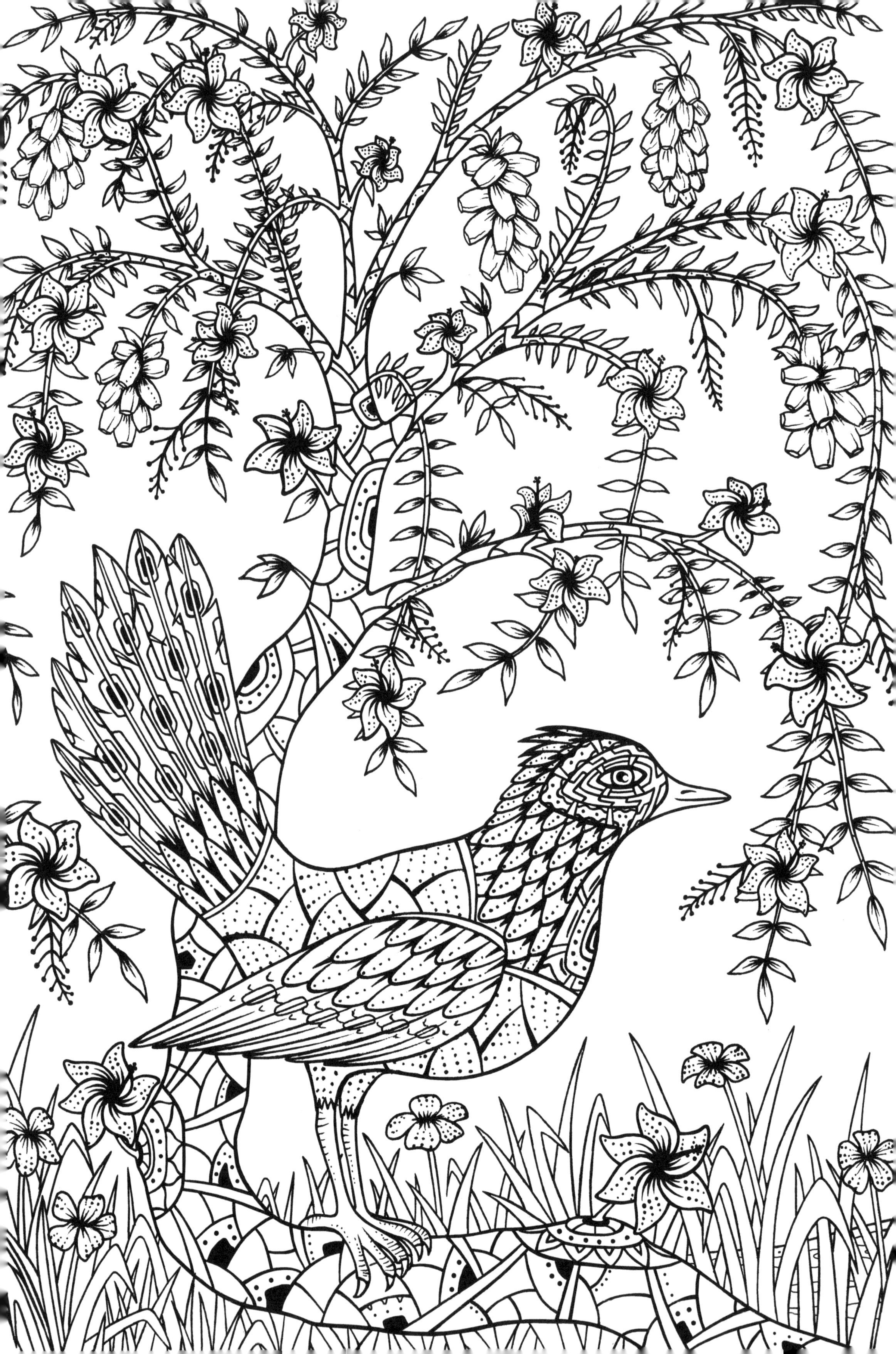

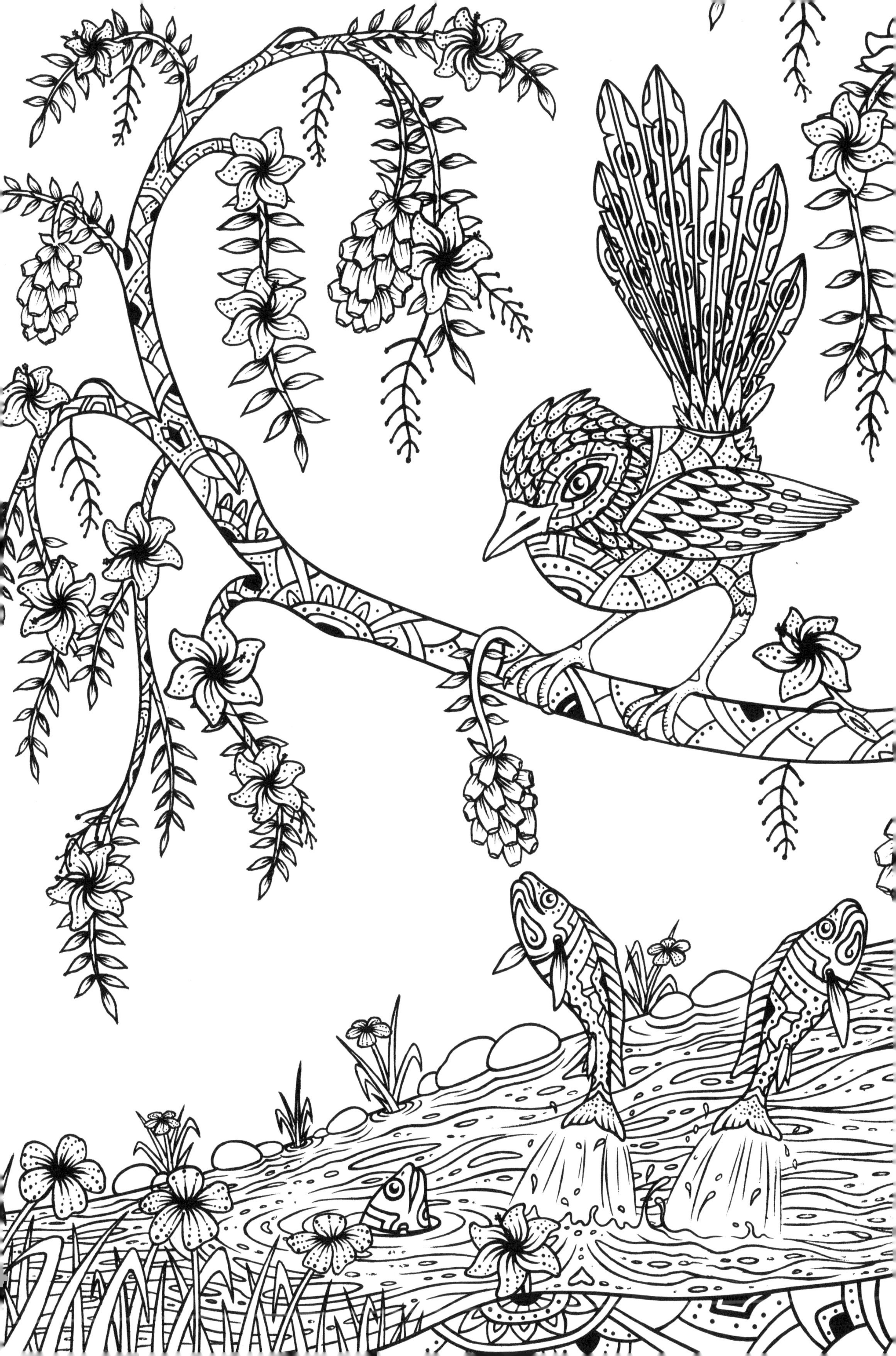

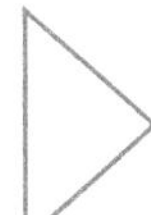

Lovebirds are nestled in the heart of a cherry grove – this panel brings the affectionate and young love of the parrot totem. Parrots are associated with love, desire and freedom of emotional expression and held sacred in many Cultural Traditions of Earth. Associated with the energies of the North and qualities like youthfulness, playfulness, affection, allure and charm, they are good totems to work with to bring more of these qualities into our life. Parrot imagery and artwork is offers valuable energetics in this capacity in the home, to help convey these related qualitative effects through symbolic association. It can relate well to the North, West and Southeast areas of the home, or walls that face these directions (meaning you are facing the direction whilst viewing the artwork) in any room of the home to lighten things up and channel parrot's affection and love. Parrots can be coloured in a variegated multiplicity of hues. What may suit well is to start with a chosen flower colour or base wood tones for the tree trunks and then complement and add coloured elements as you go. Alternatively mix bold and complementary hues together for the parrots and choose contrasting flower colours later. A third choice may be to use pastel colours for the parrots, which would work well with the fact that these are cherry blossoms and given mostly to soft pink hues. Parrot energy shows us that our emotional expression is like a language of its own and symbiotic with colour. Parrots are often given to bold and contrasting plumage and some even sporting stunning iridescent shimmers or sheens. They are associated with healing through sunshine and colour and the variegated hues of the rainbow spectrum of light. They are also associated with the expressive and communicative planets like Mercury and Venus in association with beauty, love affection and charm.

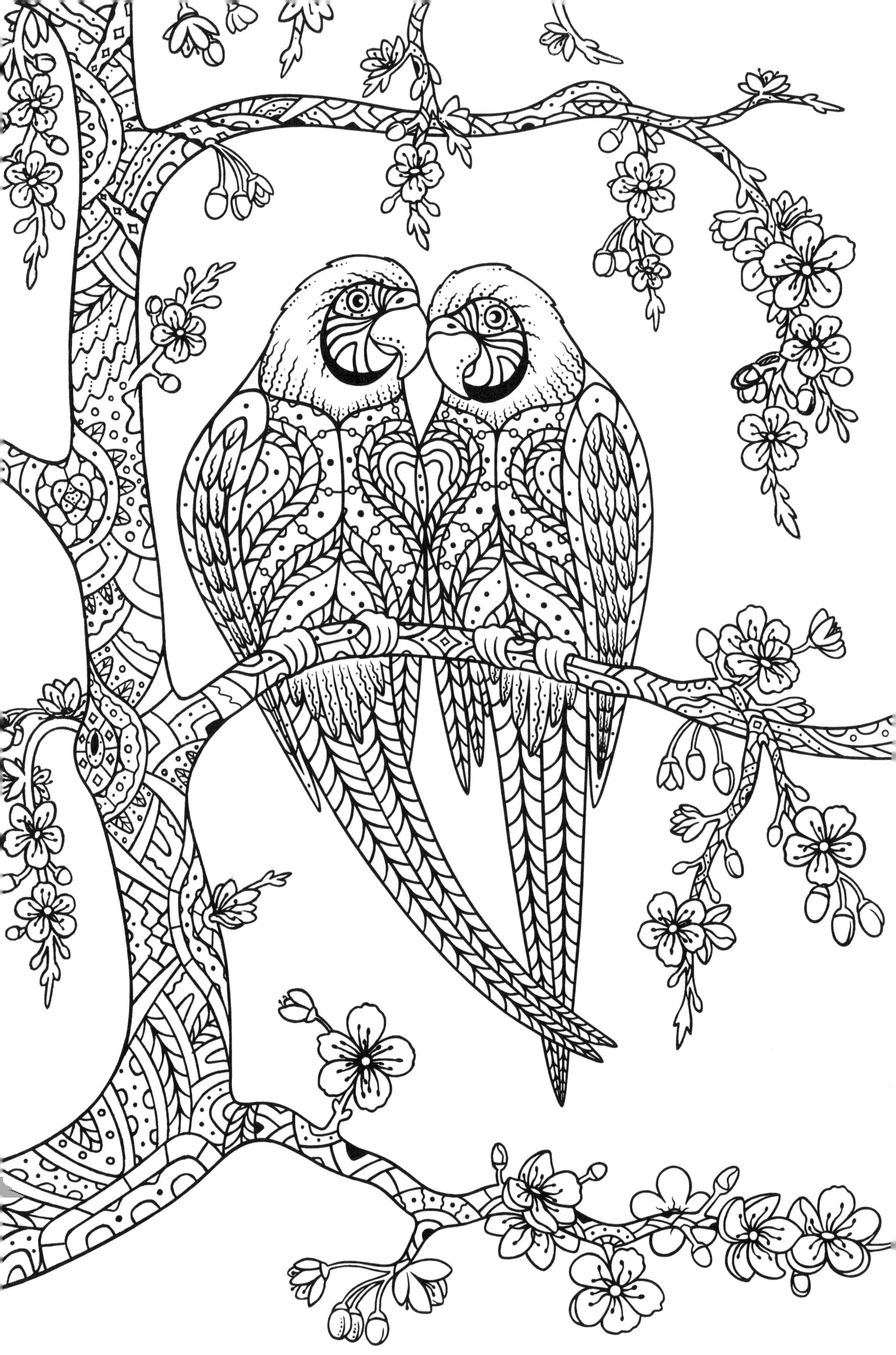

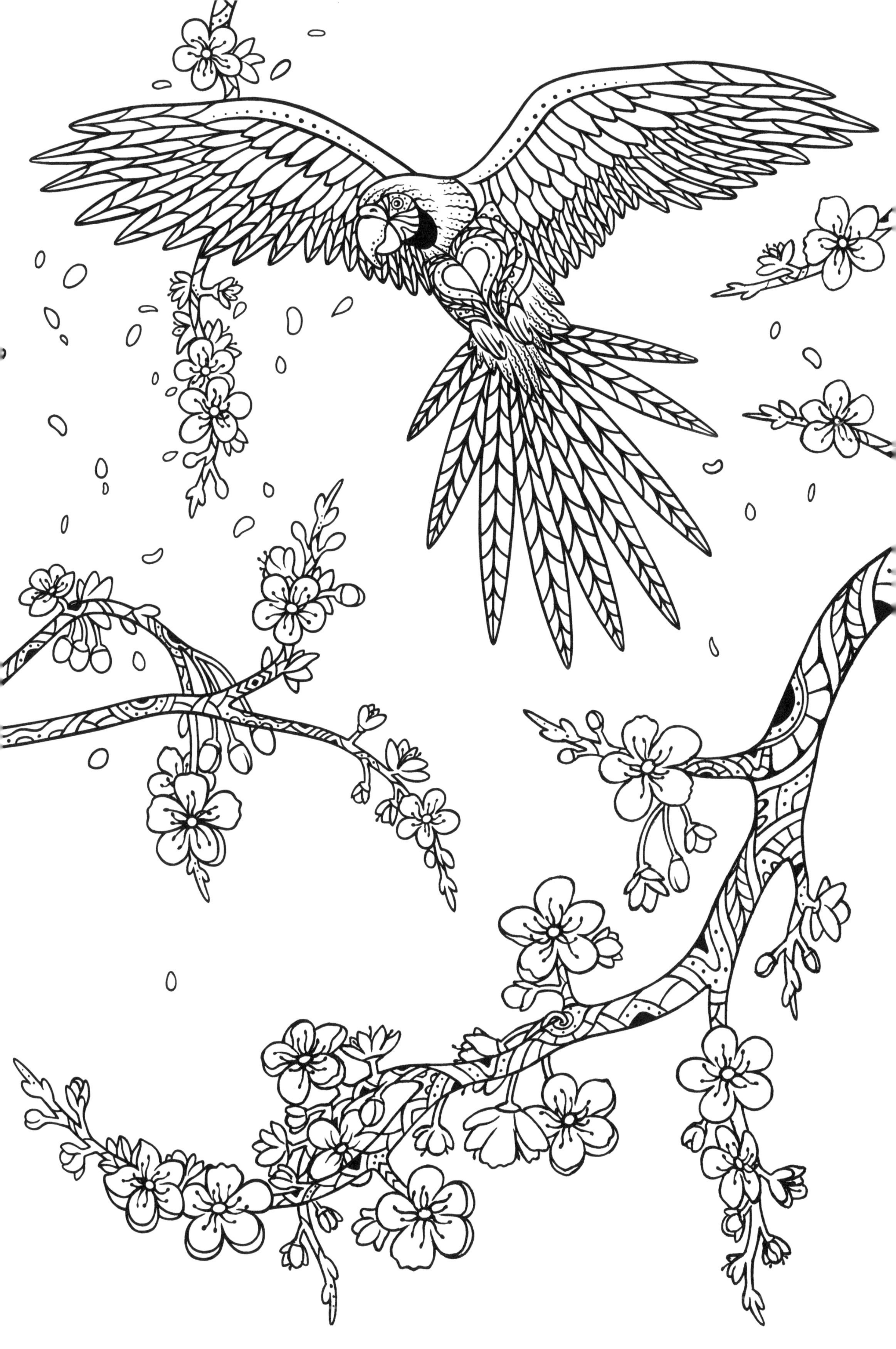

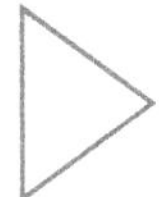

What would a day of contentment in the forest look like for a family of tigers? This in a dual-paged panel with complex symbolism indeed. The aim was first to just draw a feline tigress playing freely in the water as the first image energy or element. As the tiger totem relates to intimacy, passion and courage of the heart – in contemplation of these qualities the baby tiger cubs came to mind. They represent affection, trust, intimacy and the spirit of closeness. Tigers are held sacred in ancient and modern Indian Culture and are iconographically immortalised as the vehicle of the Goddess in her many cosmological forms. They represent qualities and traits like tenacity, ferocity, willpower, courage, integrity and inner strength.

The lagoon in the image brings in tranquil and emotional qualities, with the aquatic plants each having symbolic meaning and totemic significance. There are 5 flower species as the number '5' is associated with the goddess and her expression in material creation, which we experience through the 5 elements of nature. The flower species here each represent an aspect of goddess energy, as attributes or qualities that we can connect to through their cultural and celestial significance, and through working directly with plant energies themselves. The lotus represents here our heart being open to the light of truth, associated with the tiger totem through self conviction and knowing our hearts desires, or what brings us real lasting fulfilment. Traditionally symbolising longevity, the lotus is further associated with fortune and honour. Ideal lotus colours are pink, pastel orange or soft yellows, yet any colour may suit to complement the other flowers in the scene. Also, the various flowers can be chosen to complement the water in the green, turquoise, aqua or blue hues.

The tree flowers here are magnolias, representing timeless appreciation and enduring love. Tireless love has a tenacity about it also akin to the tiger totem. The tiger is an animal associated with Venus and the second Chakra or energy centre in the human subtle anatomy, which connects us to passion, sensuality and feelings of self-worth. The centre is the seat of the water element and relates to the fulfilment of desires, pleasure and contentment – so a water scene is fitting for the tigers and cubs. The second chakra is also the seat of creativity in its free-flowing and aspirational mode, with the cubs representing the young love, appreciation and youthful creative vigour. The flowers here are also water related, along with their qualities. The arum lily loves watery environments, spring, brooks and marshes and is associated with purity and hope. The smaller varieties known as 'calla lilies' come in a more wide variety of colours, as do tiger lilies. The tiger lily is associated with positive and radiating energetics and qualities like confidence and pride. Yellow tiger lilies symbolise wealth and gratitude, yet could be coloured in any bold and vibrant hue that represents confidence and abundance to you. Lastly there are the smaller spring bulbs bordering the lagoon, which represent new-found joy and the spring-like youth of the cubs.

Other than the observations above for the flower types, some nice contrasting colours can be achieved with this panel's artwork. For example, bright vibrant greens for the bamboo, which lends itself to shading between green hues, This works well with the signature bright orange hue associated with the tiger totem and gives the potential to create a three-part complementary effect or harmony with a variety of sky hues. Further contrast and complementary effects can be achieved with the water environment, as you have a whole host of colour options available such as seafoam green, aquas, turquoise and even indigo accents could be used. One important point to make here if for instance you choose to use blue hues for the sky, is to make it contrast the water body for best effect. For example, you could use aqua greens and turquoise for the water and then true blue with indigo shading for the sky. Alternatively, colour morning or evening sunset hues in the sky, twilight pastels, which would then allow for greater contrast and complementary effects in the water to really bring the artwork's 'colour impact' alive. There is a lot going on with this image and when in doubt on a colour choice option it is often best to leave a certain element until last and the full story often makes better sense then. In this capacity, it often becomes more clear where and why to place certain colours with image elements and artwork in the final image.

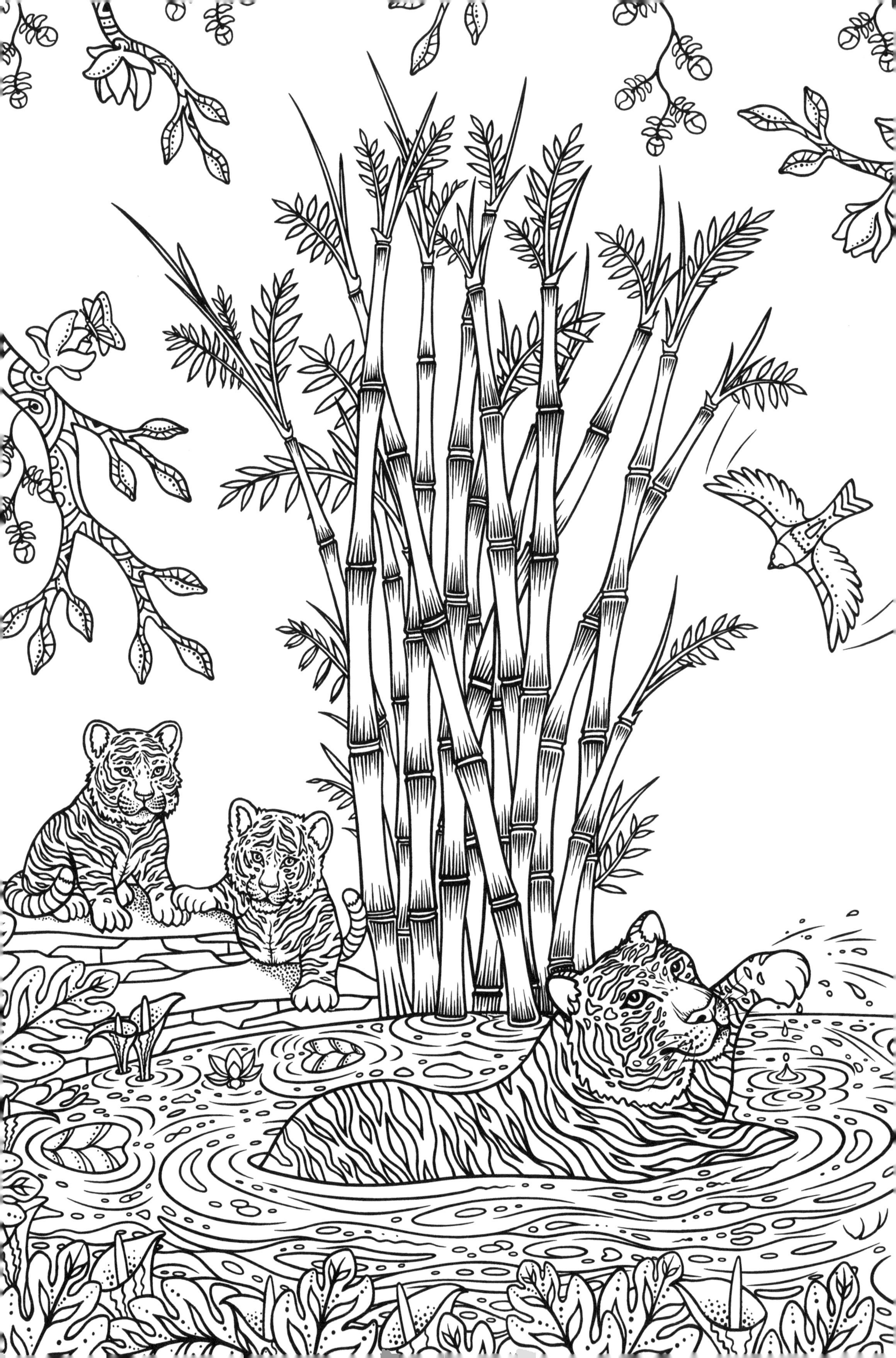

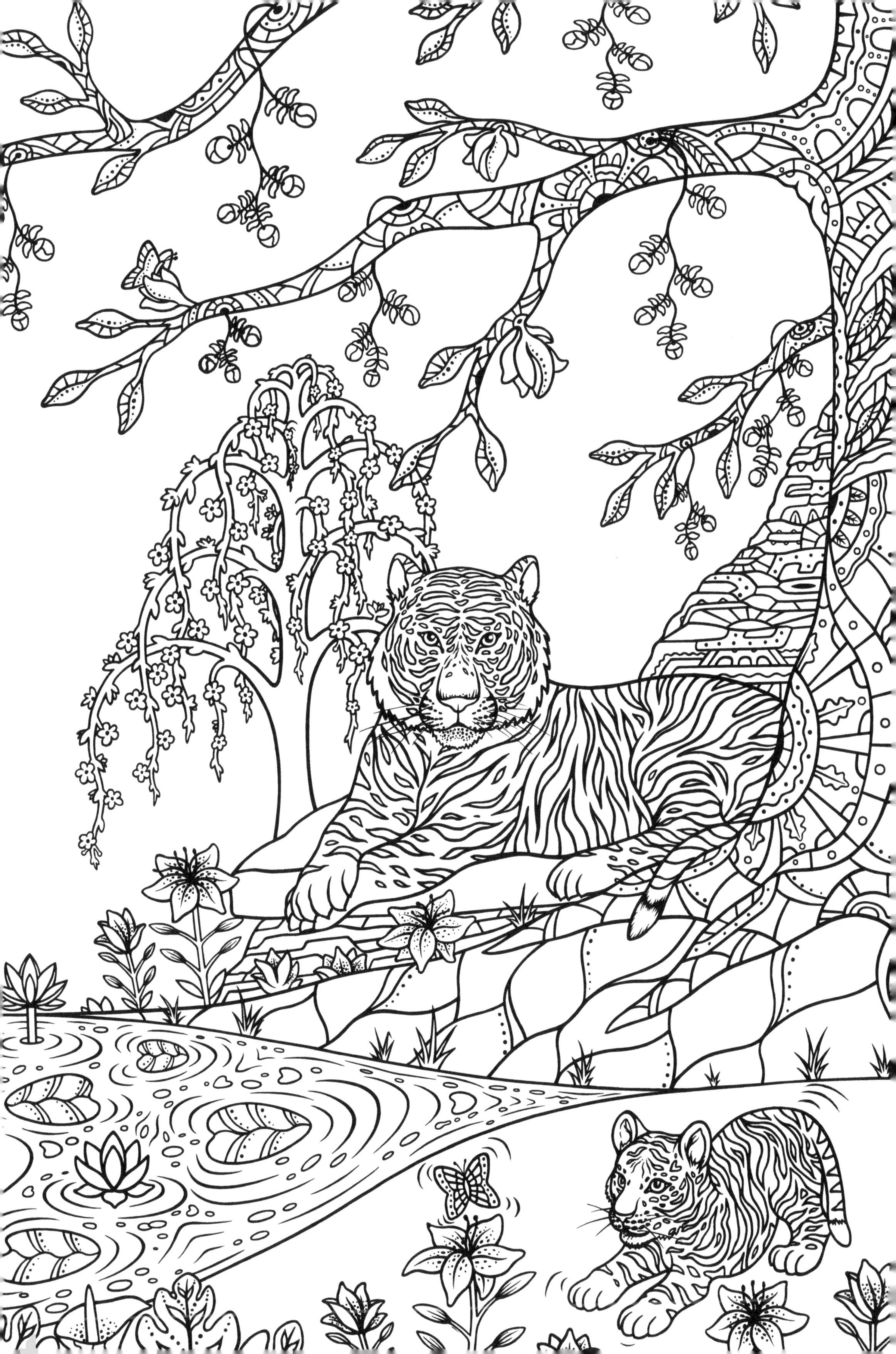

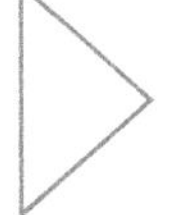

This panel is inspired by my experiences in the Australian native forests and woodlands just five minutes from home. Kangaroos are frequently seen here jumping through eucalyptus and acacia forests and cooling themselves in the shade of the surrounding creeks and waterways. A wide variety of eucalyptus trees are found here, with the eucalypt blossoms featuring in this panel along with the wattle blooms of the acacia tree. The waterfall is a feature in this Morialta Falls location, which has several falls. This one gives rainbow casts from inside or close contact to the falls. The bird in the rainbow is the forest wren, a bird which brings much life and character to this area or region. Wrens are associated with strength of character, tenacity, bold and necessary action, and the power of mental lucidity. They are associated with surmounting obstacles and challenges put before us with a sense of joy or enthusiasm. Wrens are problem solvers, or they delight in seeing solutions to problems. This is one reason why they are associated with exploration, joy and prosperity. It is also a totem associated with sacred messages, intuitive insight, charms and magical enchantment of the forest world.

The kangaroo is the world's largest marsupial and an ancient totem unique to Australia. The kangaroo holds spiritual and cultural significance to the native aboriginal custodians of this great land. They feature in many sacred dances, folklore and Dreamtime rituals of the various indigenous groups. It is associated with sacred truth and moving through the world with a sense of surrender, wisdom and wonder. The kangaroo has a gentle and innocent energy, associated with abundance and living in harmony with all living things. As semi-nomadic creatures, they generally stay faithful to a selected region or range. However they travel and forage far and wide and only take what they need, which is very different to many grazing animals that will strip a paddock clean or foliage. So they are spiritual totems associated with sustainability and responsibility and represent the opposite of material greed and consumption that we see rampant in the modern world.

Colours for this panel are largely earthy hues, though many colours may suit. Lime greens will work well, with cool green for the wattles and yellow for the wattle blooms. Pink or red works well for the eucalyptus blossoms and these hues can be worked into the sunrise or sunsets as pinks and burgundy hues. The gecko is a totem associated with dreaming, vision and the wonder of creative capacity. Nature identical colours may suit, however its totemic colours are electric blues and indigo, or even aqua suits mixed with blue. The yabbie at the bottom of the kangaroo legs in the stream is associated with the colour deep purple or plum/cool-burgundy hues. Other than this, warm yellows, golds and oranges will work well and brighten up the image, along with some fawn or tan hues, ochre, yellow-brown or rustic orange-browns.

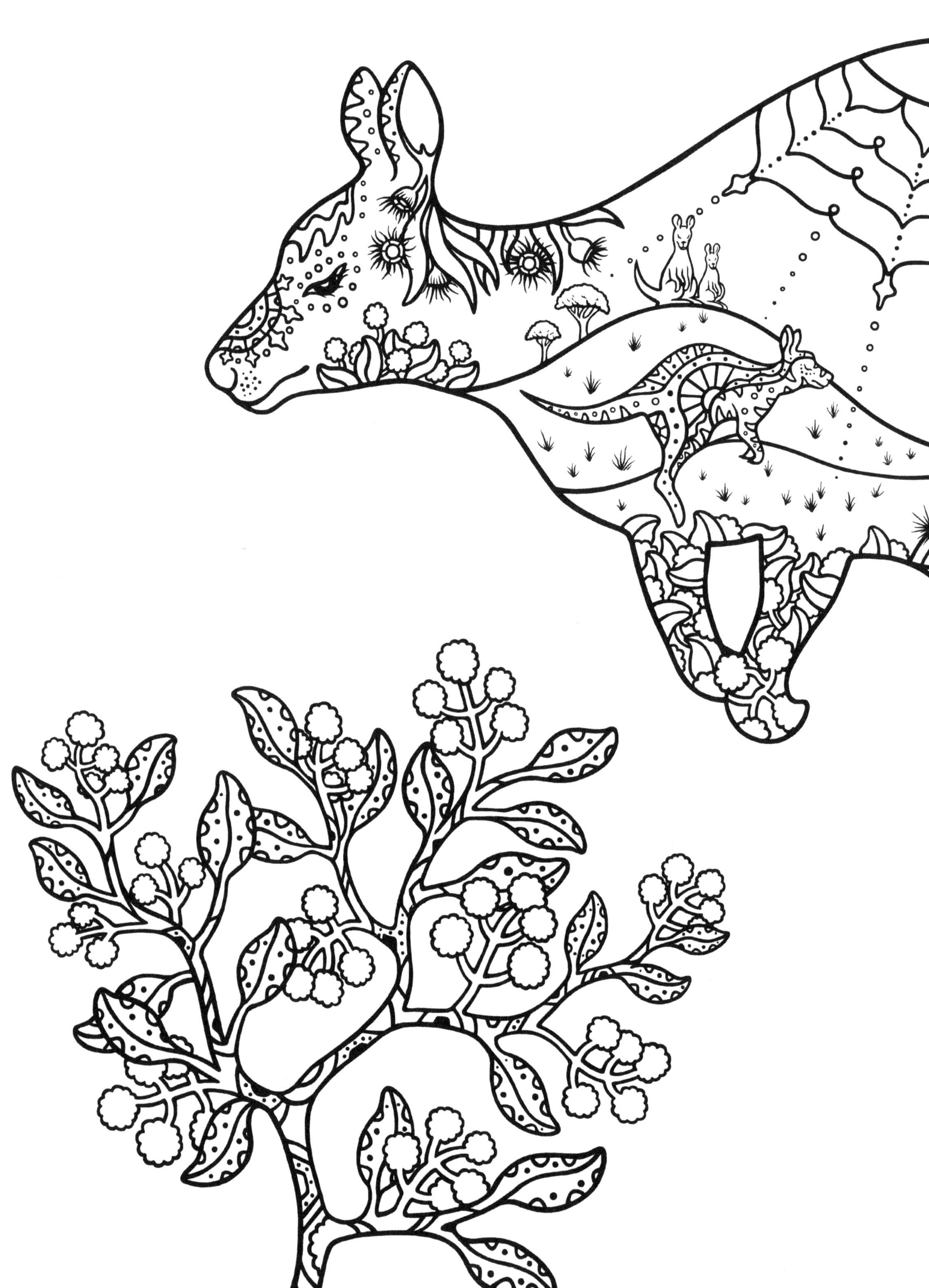

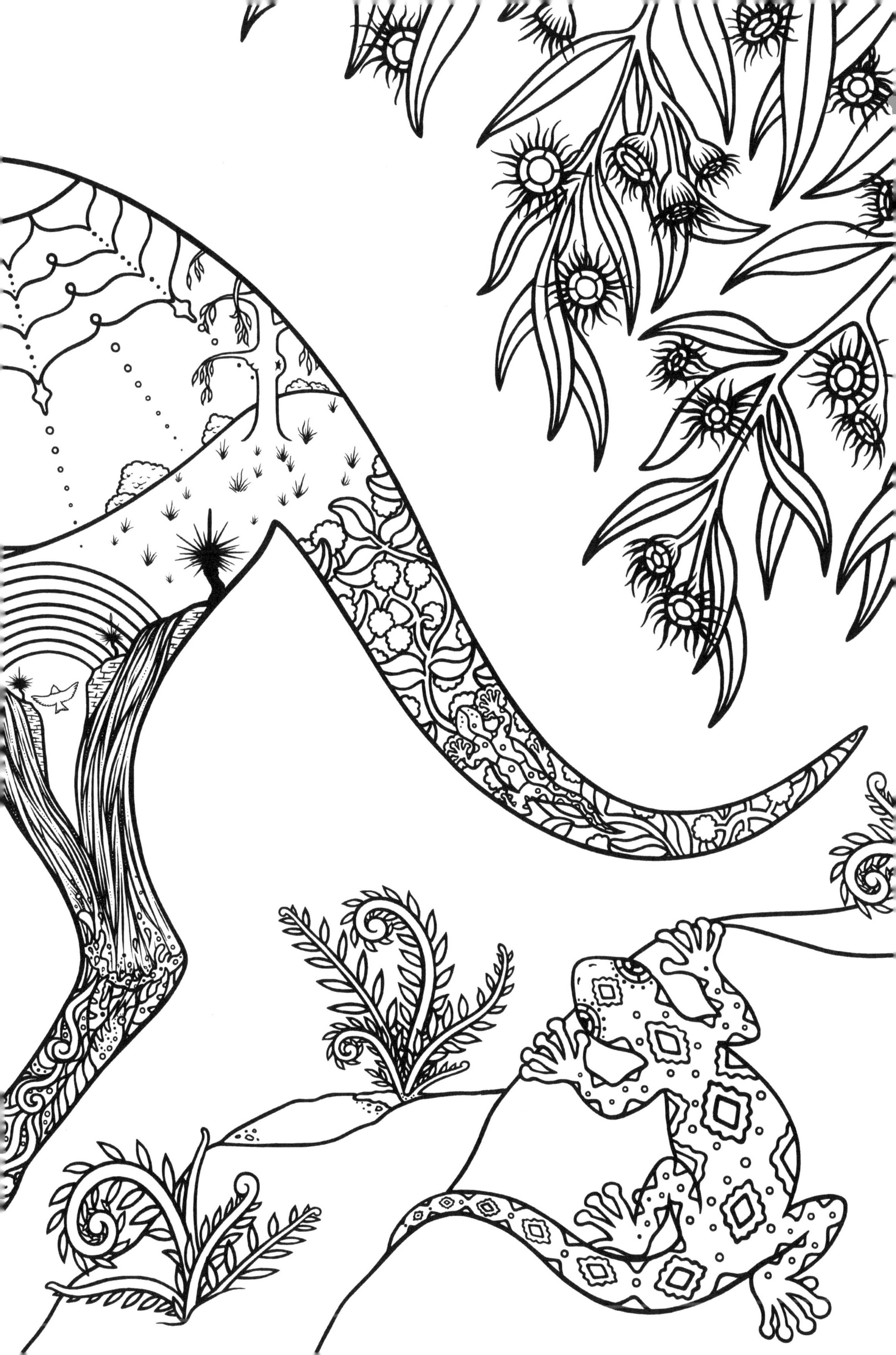

Photography for Further Inspiration and Colour Reference.

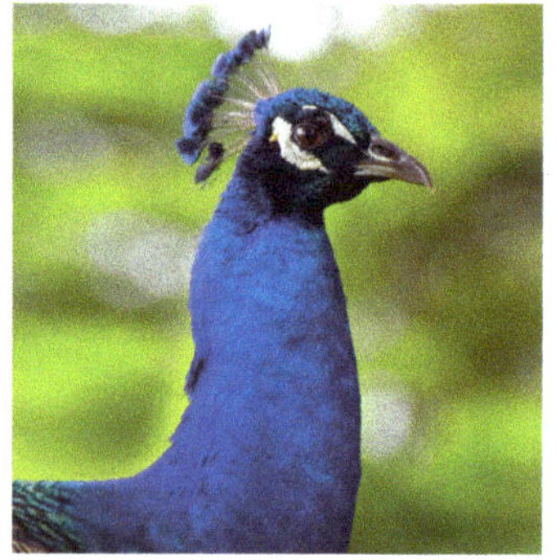
Majestic forest Peacock.

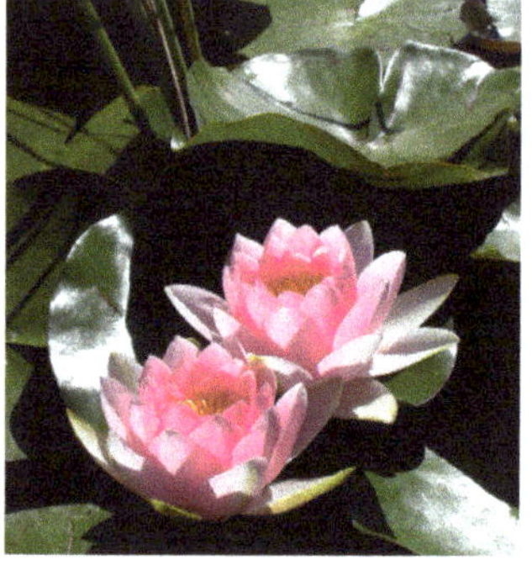
Beautiful soft pink Lotuses.

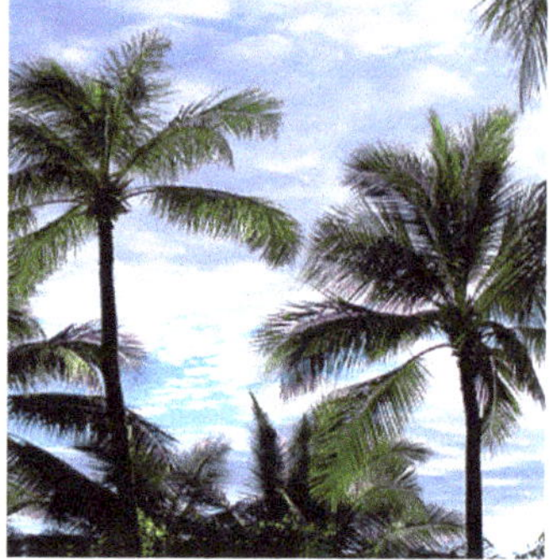
Hawaiian Rainforest Palms.

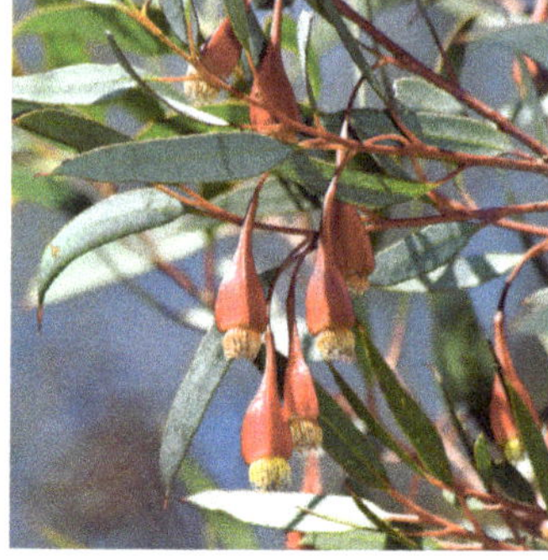
Spent Eucalyptus flower nuts.

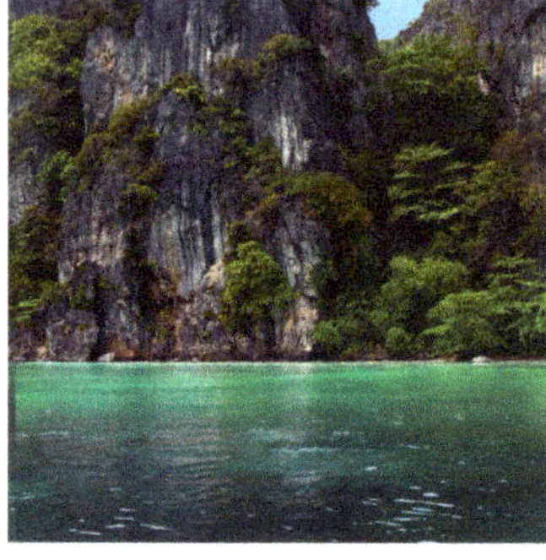
Emerald waters of Thailand.

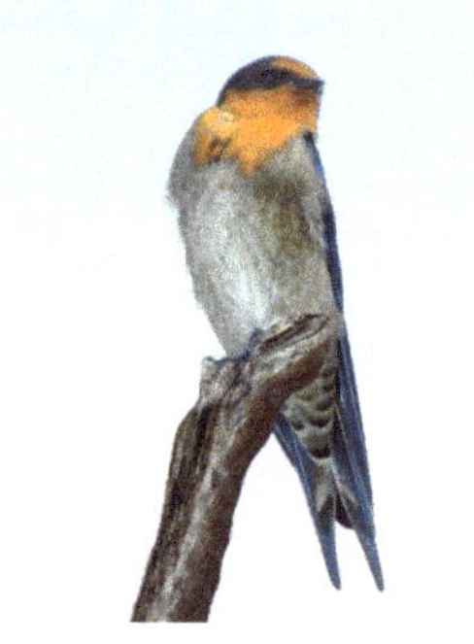
Colour variegated Swift.

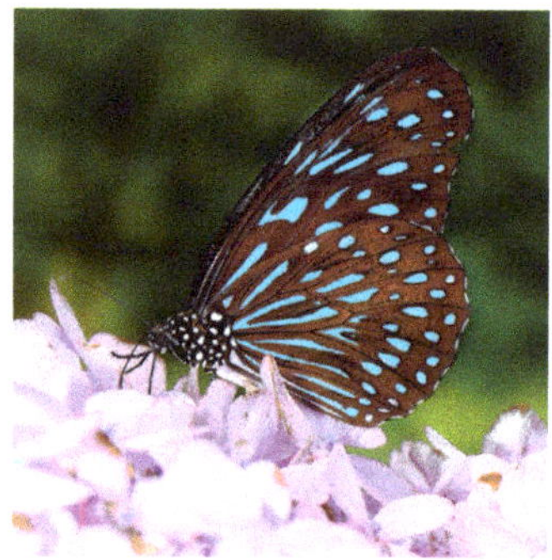
Glassy blue Tiger butterfly.

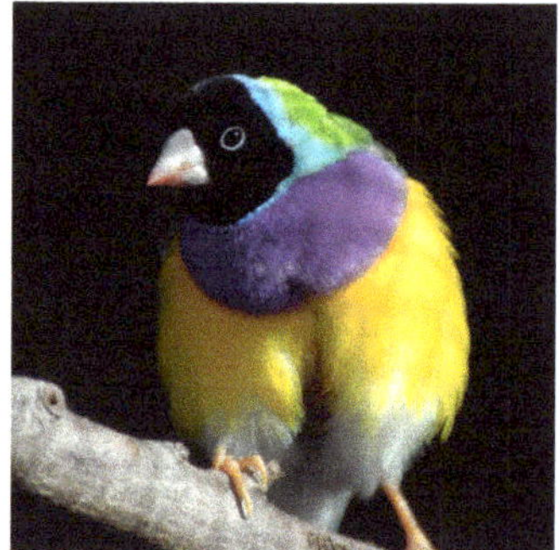
Stunning Gouldian finch.

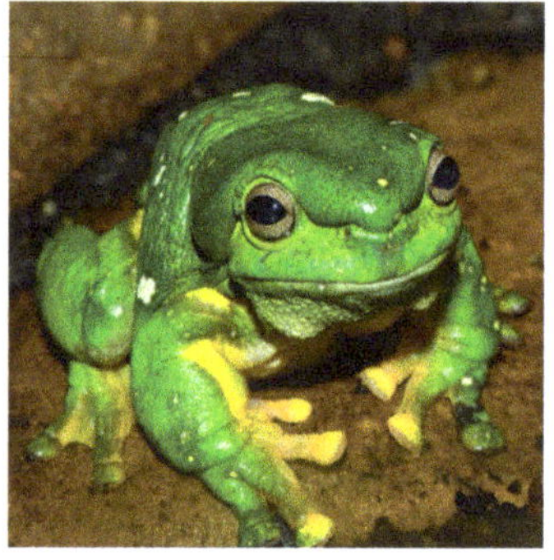
Tree Frog in green and gold.

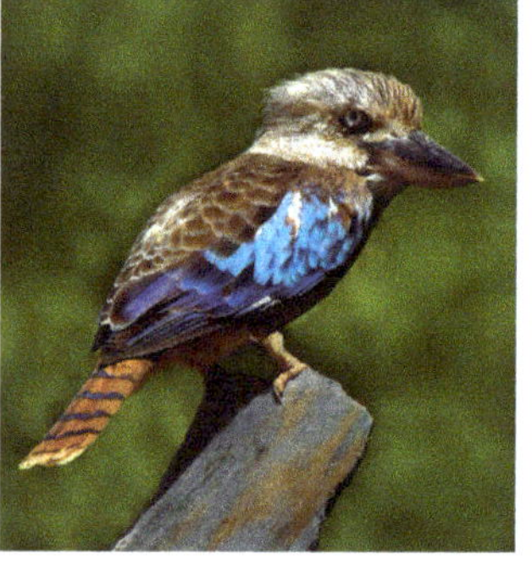
Nice Blue-winged Kookaburra.

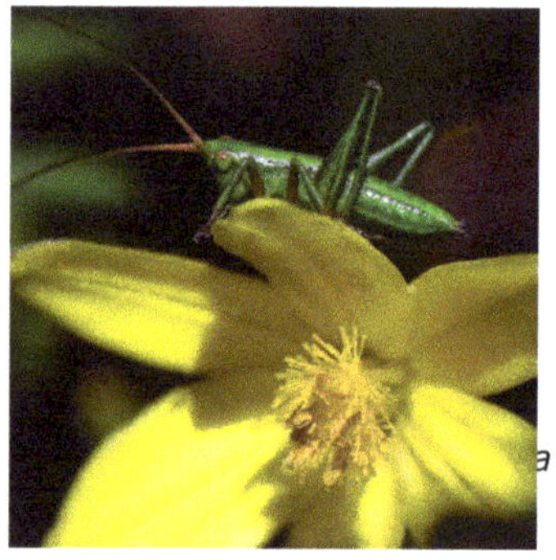
Yellow flowers bring nice effect.

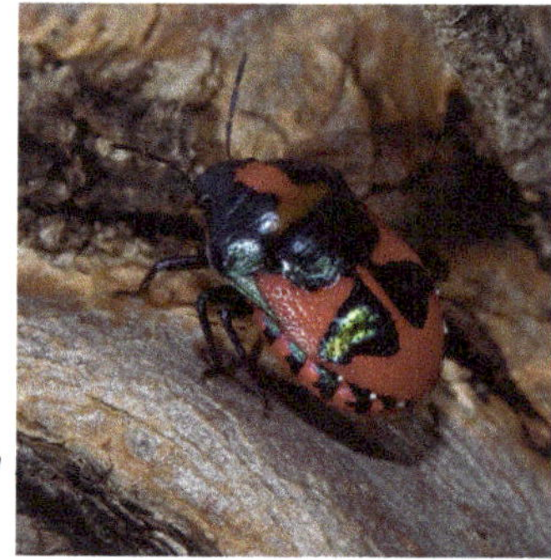
Bold colourful Jewel bug.

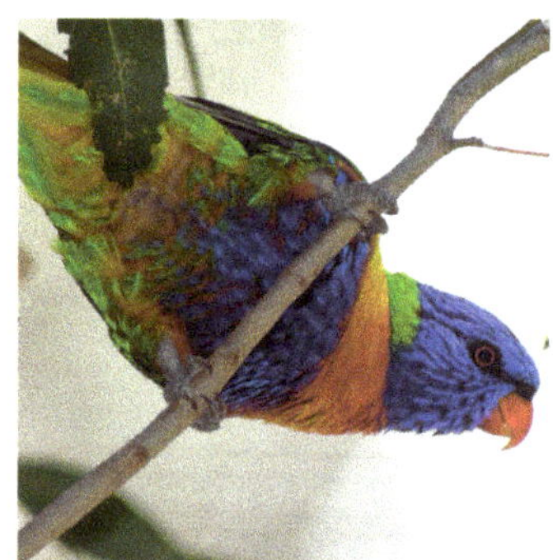
Rainbow Lorikeet with vivid hues.

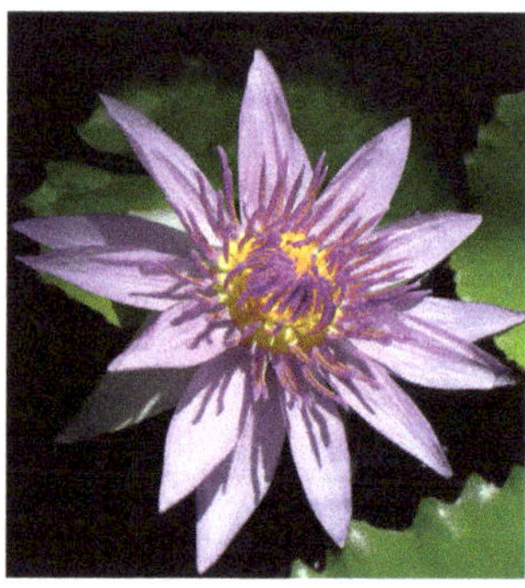
Beautiful soft lilac/violet Lily.

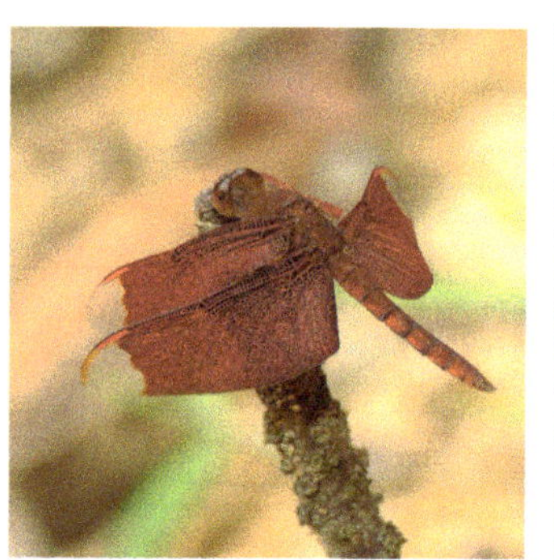
Nice red on this Thai Dragonfly.

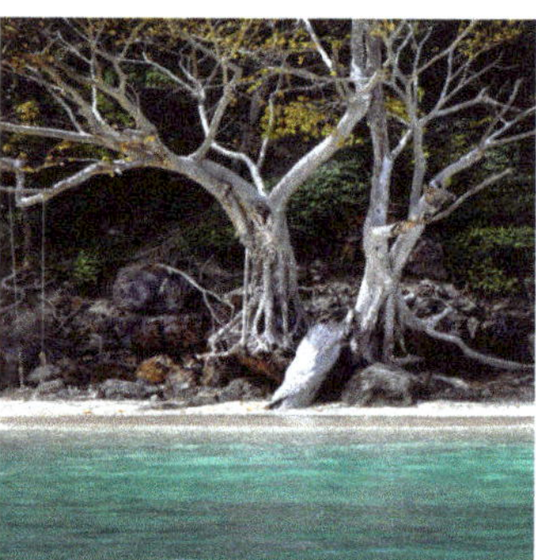
Vivid aqua from Bamboo Island.

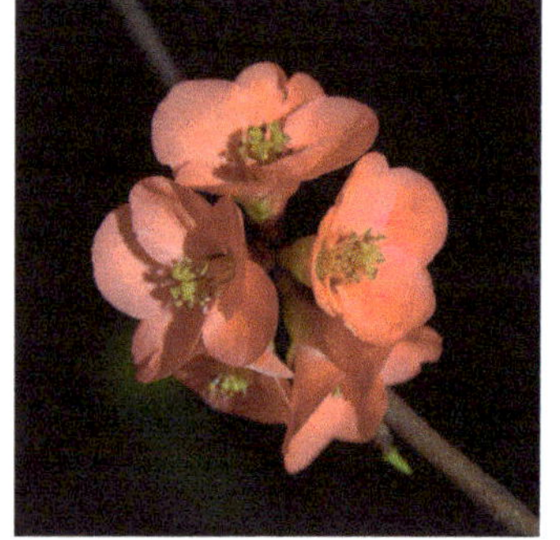
Nice coral-red Quince blossoms.

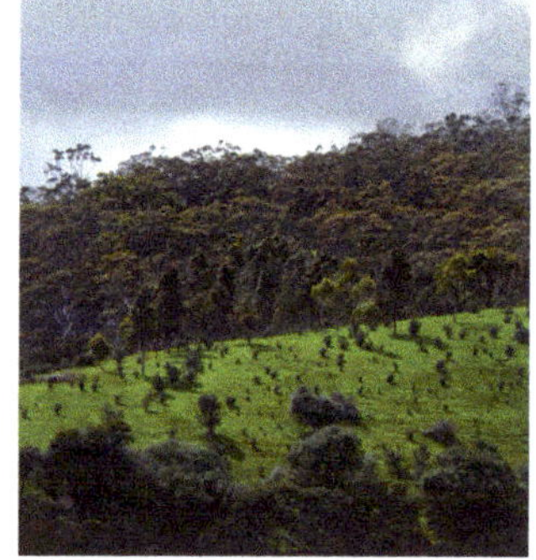
Australian Earthy greens.

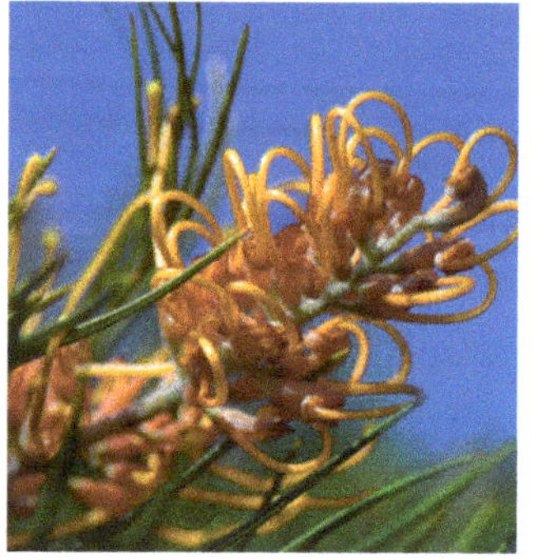
Colourful Grevillia blooms.

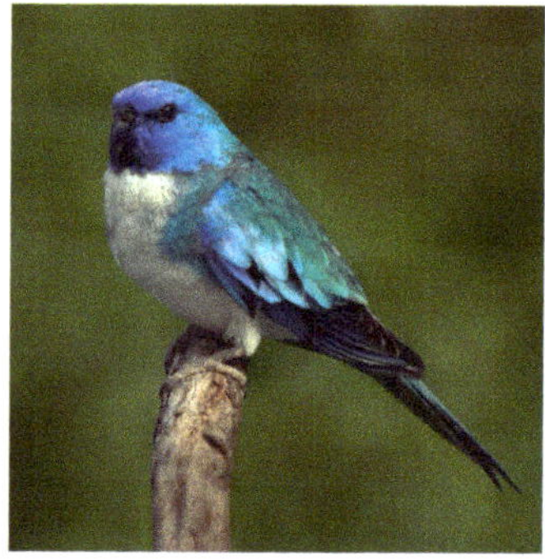
Stunning Blue-Scarlet parrot.

Below are some impactful images from my photographic library to inspire deeper colour appreciation for forest scenes. Much of the inspiration for the Masterclass Colouring Series comes from the vivid and awe-ispiring colours from the Natural World.

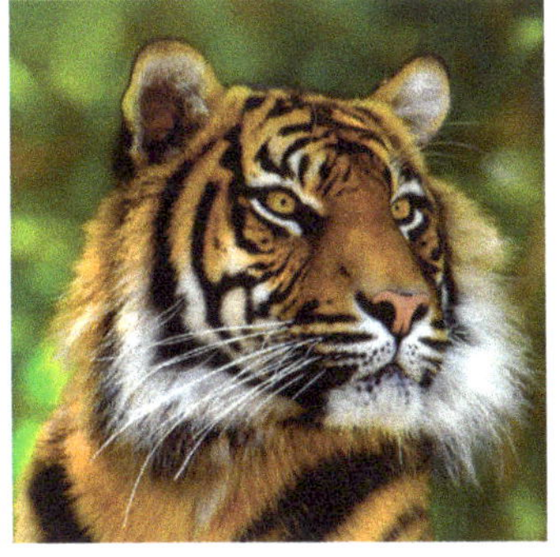
Striking contrast of Tiger fur.

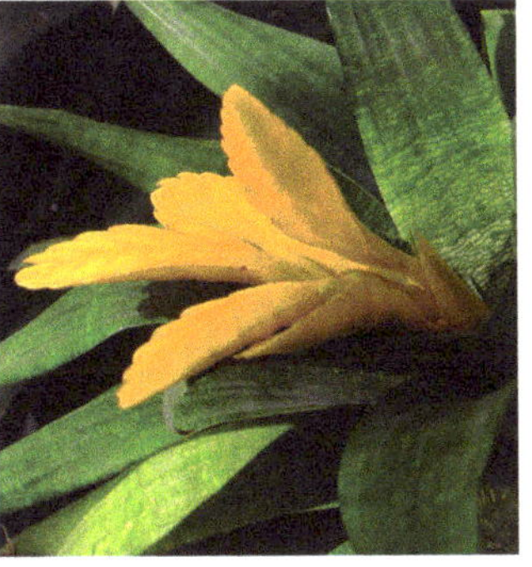
Bold yellow on this Bromeliad.

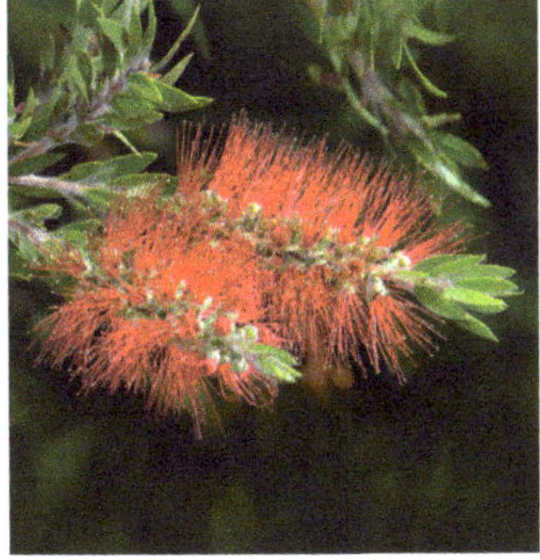
Vivid red Bottlebrush blooms.

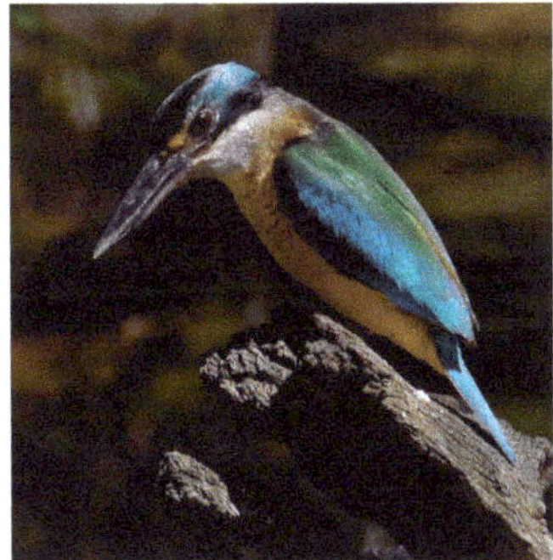
Kingfisher with Emerald & Azure.

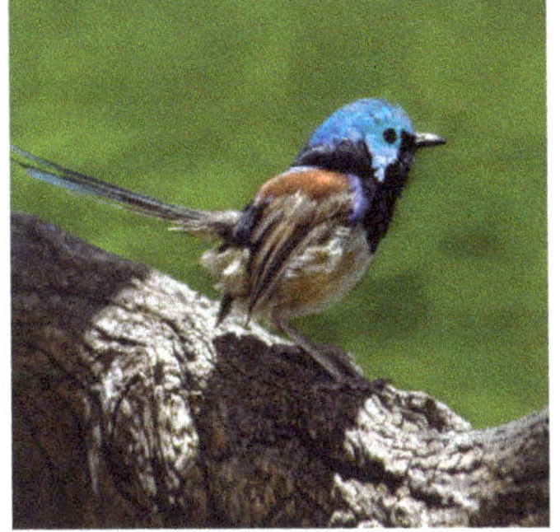
Variegated Fairy Wren.

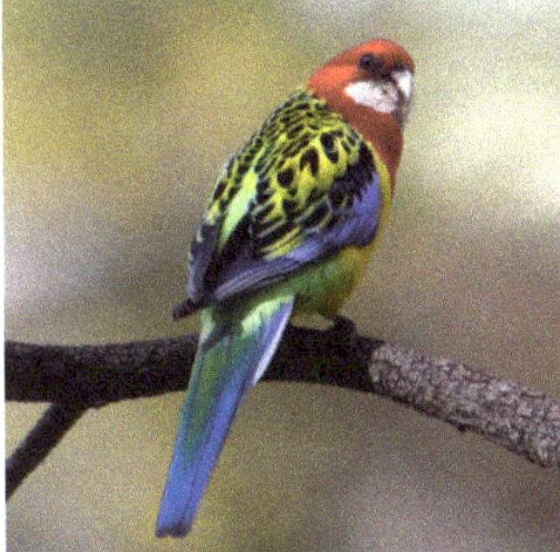
Colourful Eastern Rosella.

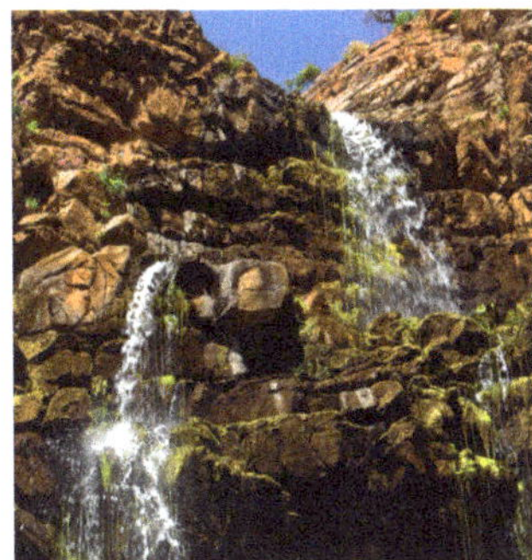
Oche-hued waterfall rocks.

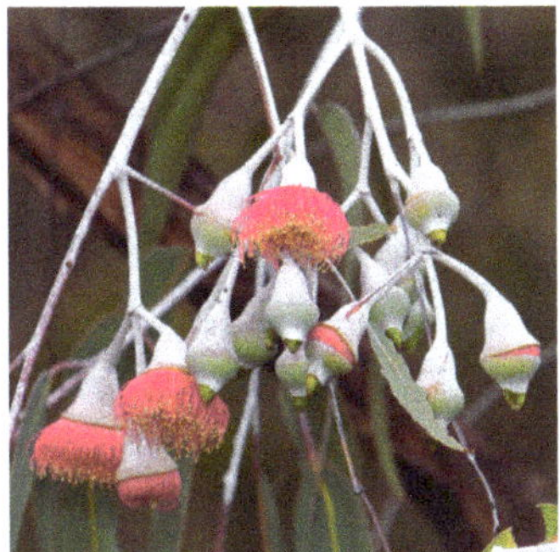
Silver Princess Gum blossoms.

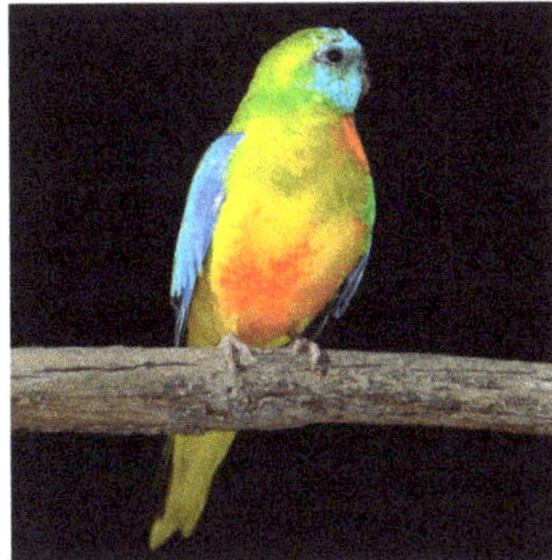
Turquoise on this 'Turquosine'.

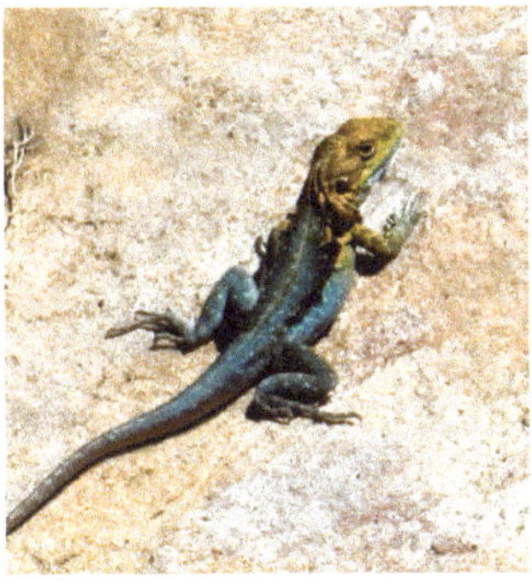
Nice colourful Amber Dragon.

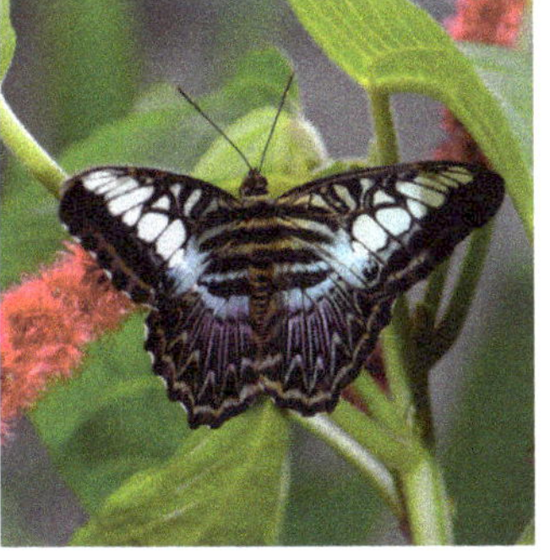
Subtle complementary effects.

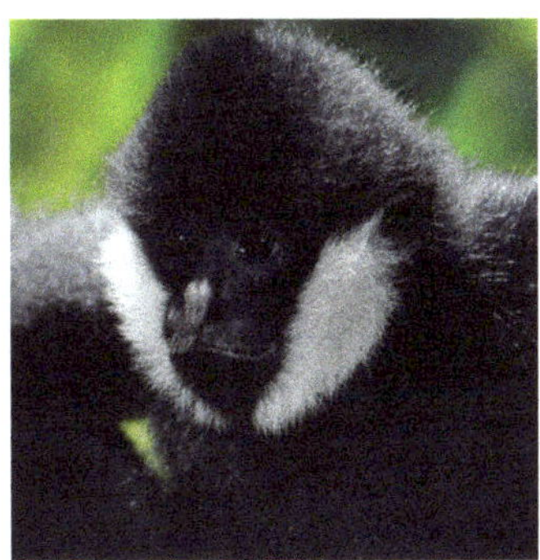
Contrast, yet no colour.

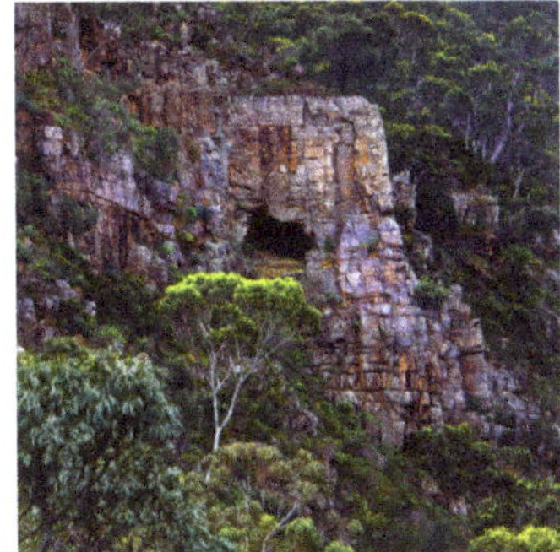
Red-stained cave in Eucalyptus.

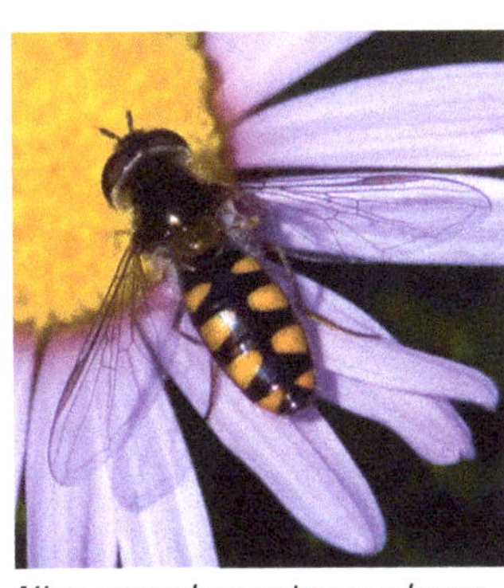
Nice complementary colours.

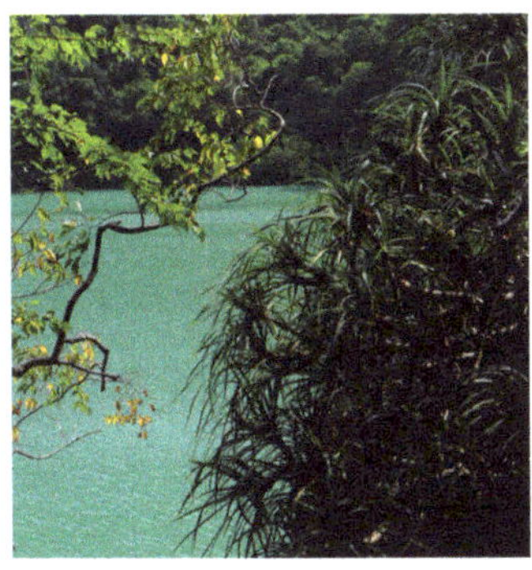
Dense forested emerald lagoon.

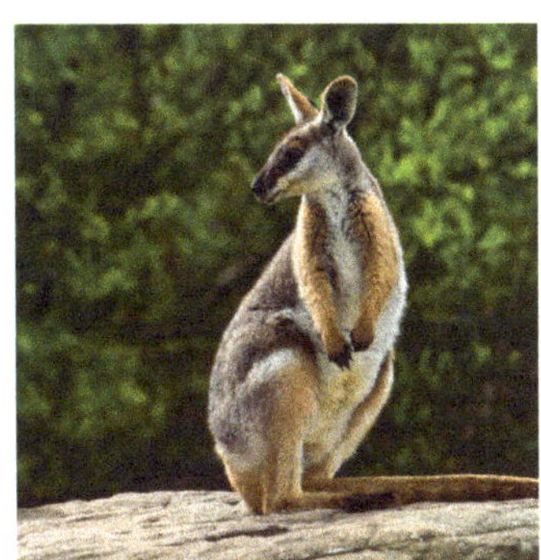
Yellow-footed Rock Wallaby.

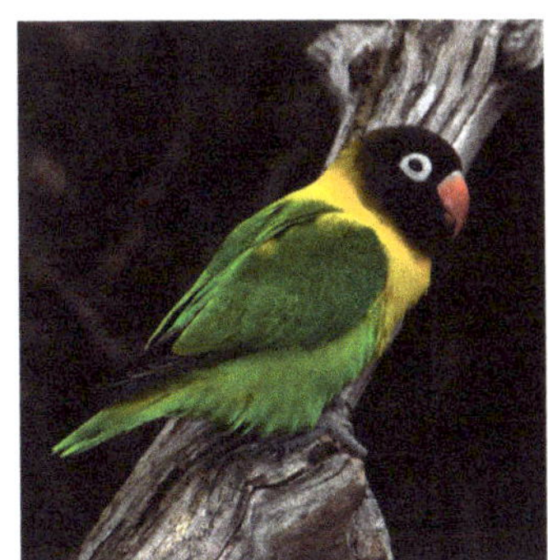
Nice colour on Masked Lovebird.

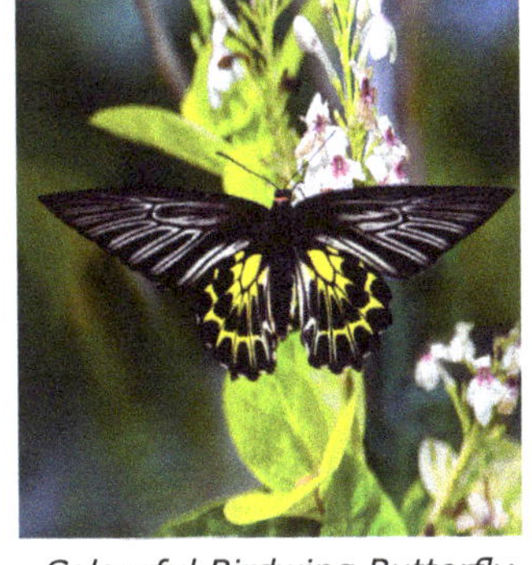
Colourful Birdwing Butterfly.

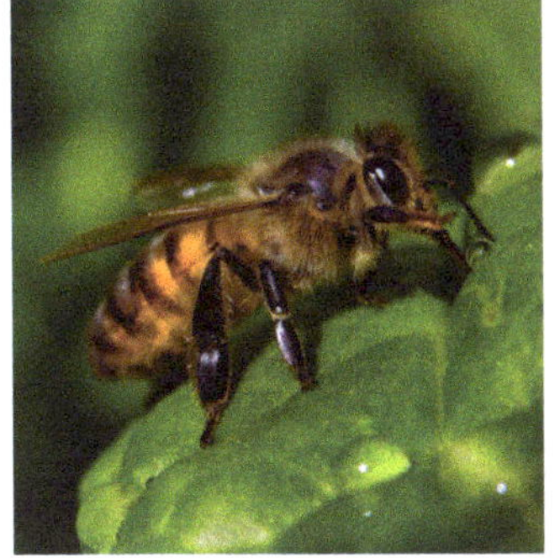
Bee drinking in the forest.

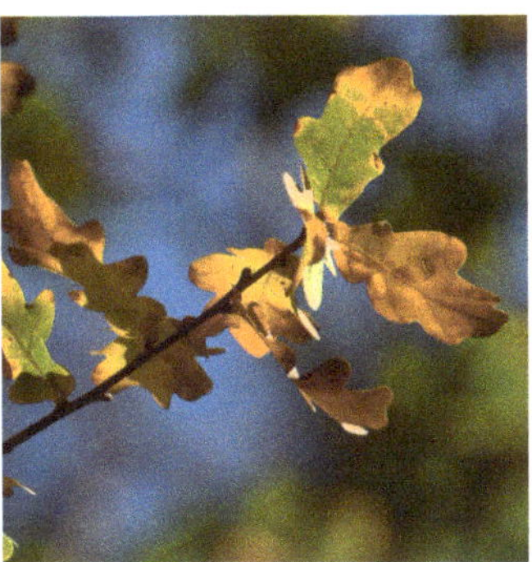
Colourful Autumn oak leaves.

Masterclass 10: Forest Animal Colours and Symbolism.

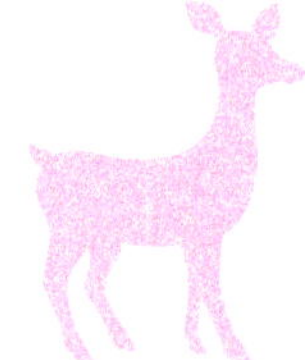

The **Deer** symbolises innocence, gentleness and purity. It is associated with the energies of the Moon and feminine attunement to Mother Nature's rhythms. The deer's gentleness helps heal hurt emotions and the wounded hearts and minds of those lost or confused. Colours are ideally white, or pink and pastel orange for refined sensitivity.

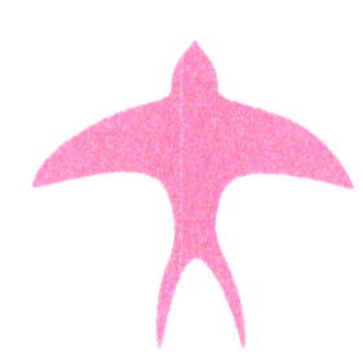

The **Swift** relates to vitalising energy dynamics and to the pink-violet and violet hues. Swifts represent harmony within restrictions of the outer world, to spreading our wings, agility and the freedom of flight. Related to the swallow, which represents welcoming energies, security, peace and preservation, qualities also of the turquoise/aqua hues.

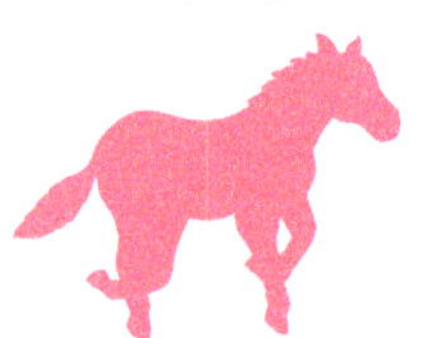

The **Horse** is a symbol of power and vitality. When associated with the sun, its appropriate colours are magenta and red. It can also embody more feminine qualities like allure and charm, which relates to Venus (white). When relating to the refinement of power, desire or sensuality, suggested colours are light violet or pastel orange.

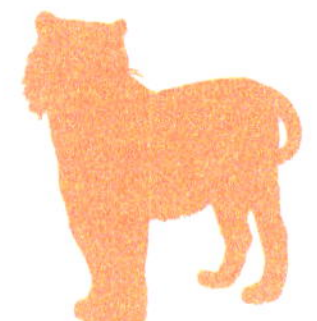

The **Tiger** symbolises passion and refined sensuality. Tigers display great motherly devotion. In the Indian tradition they are the vehicle of many goddesses and feminine deities and represent feline power and ferocity. They convey courage of the heart and the balancing of personal power. It is strongly tied with the colour orange and to burgundy or deep pinks/magentas with refining deeper desires or creative urges.

The **Bee** represents fertility, creativity and the alchemical process. Intimately connected with the pollination process and the blossoming of life. It is also associated with femininity, sensuality and mystical wisdom. Lime green and yellow hues depict the energies of spring and the principle of fertility. These colours are intricately connected with new beginnings and new life, as we see with new shoots in the plant kingdom and new spring flowers and forest blooms.

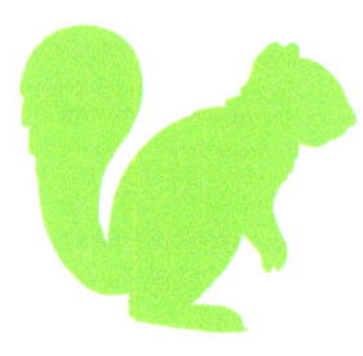

The **Squirrel** is associated with activity, play and being stocked up or prepared. The totem represents the very activity that secures abundance, hence its association with insecurity and scurrying about in search of resources and objects of need. A defined forest or woodland creature that resonates with lime green hues and light warm earthy browns. They also have an association with yellow in their sharing aspect – to the balance of gathering, distribution of energy, or giving out.

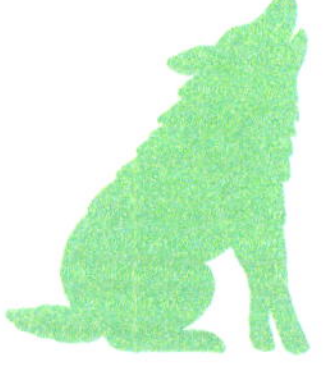

The **Wolf** signifies kinship, loyalty and trust. It relates t being sensitive to the feminine intuition and cycles of lunar energy associated in many cutures with the Moon. However, they are a 'canine' and more masculine totems, they are earthy and grounding creatures. Colours that resoante well with these characteristics and traits are greens, browns and aqua in association with kinship, or brother/sisterhood.

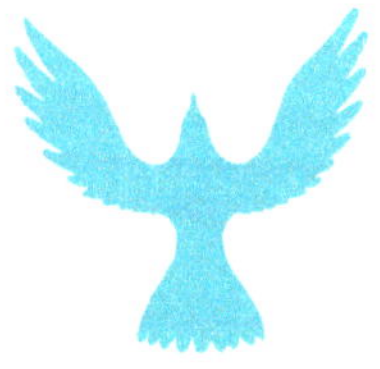

The **Dove** is universally associated with hope and peace. It suggests purity, unity, refinement and higher virtues. As a messenger of peace, it is associated with the water element and pure emotions. Invoking new life, the dove relates to blue for peace, light violet for refinement and harmony, and white for purity. The dove's connection with hope also relates to the soft or mid-blue hues.

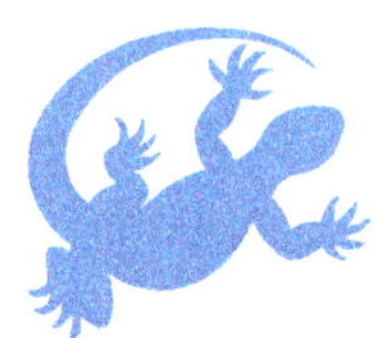

The **Lizard** represents intuitive vision and subtle perception, symbolising the balance between the waking and dreaming states of cognitive perception. It can represent a profound connection to the Dreamtime, being a valuable totem to bridge the conscious and subconscious aspects of the mind, bringing. Main colours are indigo and electric blues for foresight and vision, yet aqua colours also suit this totem well.

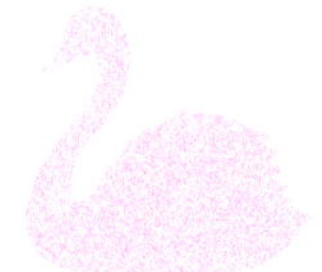

The **Swan** relates to refined qualities such as elegance, grace, harmony and purity. It is used to symbolise self-refinement and perfection. For transformation through self refinement, intuition, pure or refined knowledge it is aligned with the pink and violet hues. With water energies and purity it also relates to soft pastel blues and white.

The **Butterfly** signifies transformation of the life force from one stage to the next. A central image in the mandala, it reveals how the power of creation is transmuted. Representing freedom and new beginnings in the journey of life, its preferred colours are hot-pink and violet. Soft yellow and pastel hues can represent joy and freedom.

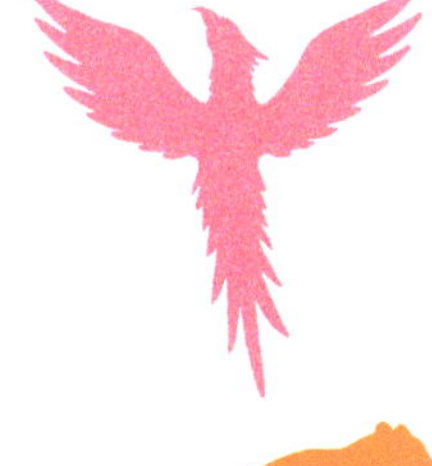

The **Phoenix** represents vitality and the transmutation of life energy relating to magenta tones. When symbolising the manifested form of power (transformation) its colour is slightly more violet than red, conveying balanced, power and completion. A good totem for manifesting and externalising creative power with the red hue.

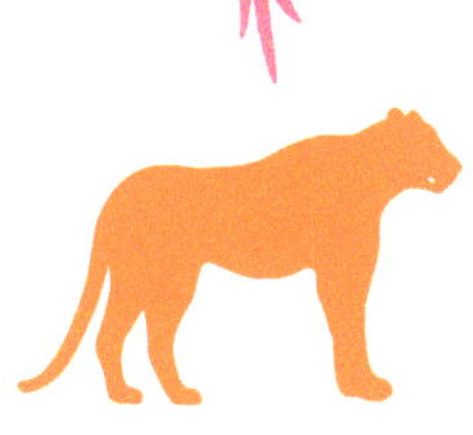

The **Jaguar** conveys integrity, courage and strength. A totem strongly associated with personal power, it relates well to orange and golden yellow hues. Cats have many totemic sub-families and here the two related would be the jaguar and leopard. These are good totems to work with if the ego or sense of will is weak, or the individual is in need of more empowerment, confidence, integrity or courage.

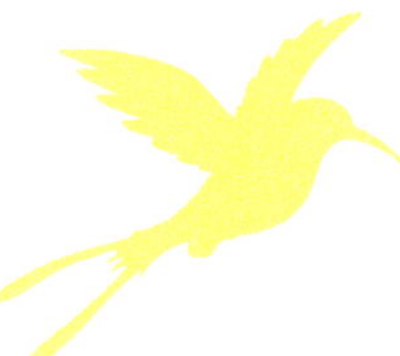

The **Hummingbird** symbolises joy and new beginnings and is great when light expansive energies are needed. It relates well to the complementary colours yellow and violet. As totems for transformation and the change from one state of creation to another, this totem can be helpful for moving through creative blocks and personal emotional hurdles. Colouring in variegated colours can be useful in this regard.

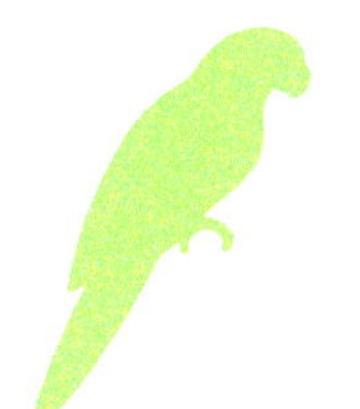

The **Parrot** is symbolic of love, romance and sensuality. Conveying freedom of growth and expression it is connected to the fertility of nature. It is associated with the energies of the goddess, and with rainbow colours with the planet Venus. Further qualities associated with the parrot are charm, affection and playfulness. Parrots are associated with the god or goddess of desire and love 'kama' in many traditions and folklore, associated here with energies of the northern direction to the colour green.

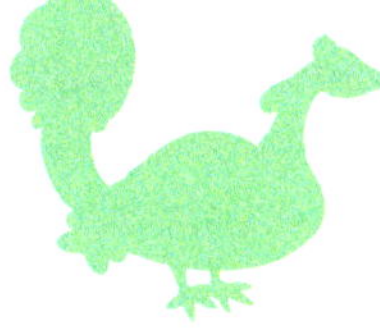

Peacocks relate to the majesty of creation and are held sacred amongst many cultural traditions. They symbolise majestic expression, glory, grace and favour. Its combined energetics can be represented by the balancing green hue, yet it can be used to represent qualities of the blue and blu-violet hues.

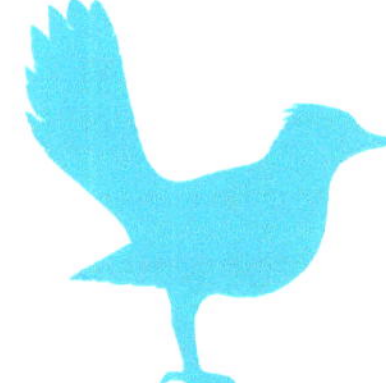

The **Wren** is associated with wisdom and messages that arise from the syntax of song verses and the deciphering of sacred sound. As a totem it is relates to the soft or mid-blue or turquoise hues in relation to invigoration and aspiration. It is also associated with resourcefulness, to bold or necessary action and to the joy associated with pure or free expression that opens new dimensions.

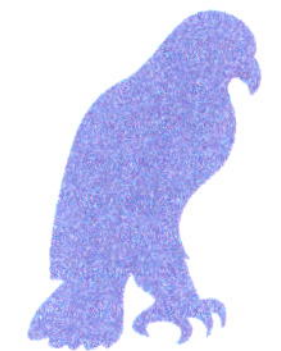

Hawks are associated with the principles of insight, foresight and greater visionary capacity. Hawks are often used to depict messengers of the heavens, gods or higher celestial realms. They are protective talismans for many and relate to varying colours depending on image depiction. Indigo for insight and revelation and gold for illuminated wisdom and the ability to have expanded awareness or vision.

Masterclass 11: Defining Colour Qualities &Tonal Variations.

The following colour guide explains the symbolic syntax and associated qualities of individual colours. Using and combining colours in thoughtful and intentional ways undoubtedly enhances your artwork.

White

Symbolises liberation and collective energy of the highest potential. It is associated with purity and the feminine planets Venus and the Moon, along with their associated element 'water'. White helps purify and pacify the emotions. White is often used to provide contrast and to bridge or shade other colours through lightening or softening their tonality. White sections in nature panels give space and heightens the energetic potential of surrounding colours.

Violet

Associated with harmony when neutral, mid-toned or slightly warm in hue. In its brighter shades it promotes transformation. As violet approaches purple it starts to become more inert or passive. Deep purple, which relates to the void, represents energy returning to its origin or source. Soft pastel violet is associated with tranquillity and equilibrium. This is a unique combination of the coming together of two opposite energies (red and blue). Violet works well for twilight skies in nature panels and for flowers, the feathers of colourful birds and for fish, anemones, corals and starfish.

Magenta (Hot Pink)

Represents the passion of the creative force (red) merged with the refinement of violet. It signifies inspiration and is used in mandalas to evoke the goddess, for colouring lotuses and to depict creative energies unfolding. Magenta is commonly used to colour triangular shapes. It is great to use in nature panels in place of red, or in an image where red may clash with other or close colours. Similar to hot-pink it works well for undersea corals, for flowers and to convey the vitality of the early morning or rising sun.

Pink

Has a calming and harmonising effect on the emotions. It promotes aspiration and helps refine deeper creative urges, as it is technically a predominance of pacifying white with a touch of magenta or red. Pink can be used to symbolise creativity manifesting gently and enhances self-refinement and sensitivity. In mandalas, pink usually represents gentle feminine energies and is used for colouring auspicious goddesses, abundance manifesting and in lotus or flower images. It can also represent the feminine aspect of the morning Sun associated with inspiration, or the Sun and Moon or Mars and Venus merged in unison. It here represents male and female balance, yet is considered to be predominantly of feminine attributes. Like magenta, it works well when needing to bring soft and sensitive qualities into an image, dawn, morning or twilight sky's, and for birds and flowers. It is very effective to use as a complementary opposite with greens and aqua hues, especially pastels.

Red

Associated with passion, desire, fertility and manifestation. In cosmology it represents the fire element and dynamic attributes of creation. Slightly cool red relates to passion, deep red to lust, or integration of sensuality and deeper desire. In association with astrological influences however, red harnesses the qualities of masculine planets like Mars and the Sun (Mars as fire red and magenta for the Sun). It is an appropriate colour for triangles, fan shapes, crescents and flames. Red can be used for passion in flowers. It represents transformation, though not essentially positive in this regard. It is great in burnt-red and cool red for defining tree branches with complimentary greens, for orchids and flowers with yellow and orange and for bold contrast in birds, fish and corals.

Orange

Used to show the gentle masculine or slightly feminine energies of the rising sun. Blended with golden yellows and pinks it represents a gentle creative force. Very soft pastel orange with a predominance of white, as we see in the full moon, represents auspiciousness and enhances maternal or nurturing qualities. Bright orange and red-orange relates more to inspiration moving towards desire. It starts to instigate Mars, the principles of externalisation and manifestation in the physical world. Softer pastels are great for adding softness to skies, refined sensitivity and bring nurturing qualities into an image. Burnt orange and deep orange tones are good for complementing other colours, for earthy scenes and some sky depictions. Orange works well for detailing trees, flowers, cats, animals, corals, fish and birds.

Yellow

Represents the expansive qualities of Jupiter and is often used to colour the outer square or perimeter of a mandala. It is used in some cultural traditions to symbolise the earth element. However this is often an esoteric association, as yellow is not aligned with the fundamental qualities of Earth (i.e heavy, gross, coarse). It often works better as amber and earthy yellows or deep yellows which become brown for earthy nature scenes. In its saffron tone it represents joy, abundance, general wealth and good fortune (Jupiter). Great for birds, fish, flowers and for contrasting and defining artwork when boldness and vibrancy is needed. Great as a contrasting complementary when used with all aquas, blue and violet hues.

Gold

Golden tones - pure gold (metallic) depicts the highest of vibrations. Relating to perfection and transcendence, it is used to emphasise shapes representing the highest virtues or most regal of qualities. It can be utilised for fine lines along with gold dots or leafing in artwork or mandalas. Gold can also be used for majestic depictions, to represent royalty and Kingship/Queenship, as we see in crests and crowns. It is considered masculine, bold, highlighting and good for defining borders. Used to emboss image elements and stylised lines in artwork for an expensive or regal effect. Gold in the colour wheel (Fig. 2) can be used in place of metallic gold and suits spring flowers and sunrises.

Lime

Is used to invoke fertile and activating life-giving energies. It relates to new growth and the vitality of spring. Lime can be used in gardens, or the outer square of a mandala for active and communicative life energies, where it conveys invigorating qualities. Use sparingly, as lime has a vitalising and stimulating effect and too much can be overpowering in artwork. It complements well with violets, blues and aqua, yet clashes with red and somewhat with red-orange.

Green

Is linked to lime. Green fosters communication, preservation and exchange. It reflects properties such as growth and fertility. As vibrant mid-green it depicts interconnection, with the cooler emerald or blue-green shades conveying calmness or balance. Green is often used to signify the air element and the equalising attribute of nature, as it can be either warm as lime green (slightly active) or cool as emerald or aqua-green (slightly passive). It suits detailing leaves, grass, seagrass and foliage, yet can also be used for many animals and nature settings. Parrots relate well to green and lizards such as geckos and chameleons. Great for using in various shades in forest and water settings. It contrasts well with browns, blues, aqua and violet. Relates to planet Mercury.

Aqua

Effective when working with higher expression of the emotions, for communicative energies in general and pacifying intense emotions.
It helps calm or soothe more intense

aspects or our self-expressive capacity. Great for water settings and animals that depict peaceful and playful energies like the dolphin, otter (sisterhood/brotherhood) and some birds like parrots, falcons and hawks.

Aqua-greens are good for the air element and represent the principles of intercommunion and sustenance. They work well with contrasting colours like gold, amber and orange when it suits the artwork and story expression being defined or created. They can be used instead of cyan blue or true green if they better suit for complementary effects, as this is technically a bridging hue between these two colours. Can be used in forest and ocean scenes to great effect and for subtle detail in birds, foliage, corals and flowers.

Aqua-blue means more blue than green. This hue can relate to the water element and the flow of our emotions and creative expression. Turquoise fosters freedom of artistic expression and refined sensitivity. It suits the elements of air and water. Aqua colours are favoured by artists for these reasons and can work well with indigo, violet and light brown or tan colours. They also complement black and can be used to lighten up or take the edge off of black's otherwise heavy or restrictive qualities. Great for parrots lizards, ocean and sky settings and for contrasting yellow and gold-orange.

Blue

In its lighter and pastel tones blue is similar to aqua and can be used in nature settings and mandalas to represent gentle passive or peaceful qualities. It is used symbolically to represent the air element as light to mid pastel blue, which promote openness and expansiveness. Mid blue relates to the gentle and refined expression of energies. It relates to the sky from light, through to mid blue and relates well to peaceful birds like parrots and doves. It can also be used to symbolise the ocean, as ocean water reflects the blue of sky. As it starts to move toward warm blue or deep blue its energetic attributes change considerably. Here we start to get qualities suitable for deep oceans or the night sky as with the deep blue and the indigo hues.

Indigo

This hue is half way between blue and purple, yet often on the blue side or considered 'warm blue'. Indigo relates to the principles of insight, wisdom, wonder and revelation. It can be used to represent depth in an image and for ocean and night sky settings. It also relates to the principles of structure and mental integration. It complements well with aqua, green, yellow and orange hues. Indigo represents purposefulness and structural integrity and is utilised when defining boundaries. The most invigorating of the blue tones when not too dark. It relates to creative vision. In its deeper tones it encourages insight into life's more contemplative mysteries.

Purple

Somewhere between indigo and violet, purple is considered closer in energetic qualities and effect to indigo. Purple is neutral to cool and somewhat negating in effect. It is good for creating depth in an image and for defining boundaries. It relates to the integration of opposites like the meeting of red and blue (pastel-lavender for gentle integration). It can be used in night and deep sea depictions, or for colourful birds, flowers, gems or minerals and to add depth to skies. Deep purple has similar qualities to deep blue.

Deep Blue

Neutral and passive in its mid-tones, yet as blue starts to become darker, it relates more directly to passiveness and inertia. This colour can be depressive in large amounts or environments, as it harnesses the limiting and retarding energies of Saturn. In traditional sacred art, dark blue is often used to represent the qualities of inertia, structure and contraction. Deep blue also relates to the principle of withdrawal, or receding and connecting with the life source vibration. It represents birthing and conception in this regard, creativity taking form and the gestation or womb state of creation.

Black

Defines the light and all other colours. It is used in mandalas for border designs and boundaries, representing structure. It represents qualities like negation, subtraction and devolution. It is also associated with the heavy and gross qualities of the earth element (Saturn). Black can be used to depict negative or wrathful energies, inertia and darkness in general. Not truely considered a colour, yet used more for its energy-negating or defining effects for boundaries and foundations.

Black can also work effectively to create small null spaces or void sections in artwork, or that contain the overall artwork. It can also represent fear and may be used in small carefully placed areas in artwork when moving through difficult personal junctures, or emotions like grief or sorrow. It can also be useful with companion colours like aqua, gold and cool violets when working with the shadow side of the psyche. It represents the mysterious, the limited and the unknown.

Grey

In its mid smoky tone, grey is used traditionally in chakras/mandalas to depict the 'ether' element . Light smoky tones are also associated with the air element, and relate to unseen, veiled or invisible energies. Used in the mandala it signifies both beauty and perfection as light, neutral or soft cool-greys. Grey can also be seen as a shade of black and when shading can be used as per black in its darker grey shades.

Blue-greys can represent unmanifest forms, the conception of form, or an element of turbulent or abrupt change, as in the colour of storm clouds. Lighter blue-greys can be used for a complementary effect, or for areas or designs that call for gentle contraction or undefined qualities manifesting, or that are in a state of flux. They provide somewhat relaxing or soothing effects. Not by themselves though, yet better mixed with vibrant greens, bright blues, pinks/violets, yellow or gold.

Brown

Symbolises the earth element in its most basic association, especially dark browns which represent heavy, static or solid foundational energies in artwork. Brown can be used effectively in colouring trees and nature panels, yet with caution as things can get muddy or dirty depending on the design.

Red-browns are good for colouring squares, grounds and outer perimeters of drawings and designs. They mix well with yellow, orange or gold hues and even warm violets and pinks. They represent the principle of manifestation and become warmer with reds, pinks and violets added. Deeper browns with added golden browns or amber hues are more earthy, grounding or complementary. These hues also work with squares and triangular shapes and earthy animal totems like the ram, snake (earth snake), bull or horse. Good for earth minerals and crystals, for general colour relief and for fruits, flowers, berries and native fauna.

Green-browns, Tan are great for nature scenes, providing they are not too dirty or muddy. Mid green-browns and mid/light brown (tan) hues are great for colouring images that relate to nature, growth, or the principles of practicality and sustenance. They work well with other green, aqua, blue and purple hues. Muddy browns and swampy tawny green-browns however represent wrathful energies in nature, like we see in the army-green colours.

Darker or tawny green-browns are traditionally used to show destructive energies or wrathful forces in sacred art. Relating to murky colours such as a swamp, they promotes turbulent or chaotic energies. These hues should generally be avoided unless in small amounts to create dramatic tension in an image or to divide a segment or area of a panel. They can alternatively work well with swamps, mud, trees and leaves and compliment well with aqua, blues, violets and golden hues.

Masterclass 12: Complementary Colour Usage - Shading & Toning.

Complementary colours can be used in many ways in our artwork, images and designs. The traditional approach may be to use complementary opposites, which work well when contrasting effects are in need. The use of complementary opposites in artwork also helps restore equilibrium to the left and right hemispheres of the brain, which brings greater scope for a whole range of potentially beneficial and remedial effects.

Also, the term 'complementary' may apply to colours that complement each other for a variety of reasons. A dusty or slightly muted-pink for example, complements purple and violet, as we see in a majestic sunset. Golden yellow may be employed to complement its brother or sister hues of orange and red. So there are many ways to employ complementary colour usage with specific effects in mind.

To help further enliven your colouring journey, the following base colours are a general guide for opposites and supportive complementary effects :

Supporting Complementaries -

- Magenta, Red, Yellow, Orange.
- Turquoise, Aqua, Green & Lime.
- Cobalt, Cyan, Turquoise, Green.
- Purple, Indigo, Blue, Cyan.

Complementary Opposites -

- Purple/Indigo <>Gold/Yellow.
- Violet/Magenta <>Green/Lime.
- Green/Aqua <>Vermillion/Red.
- Blue/Cyan <>Orange/Red.

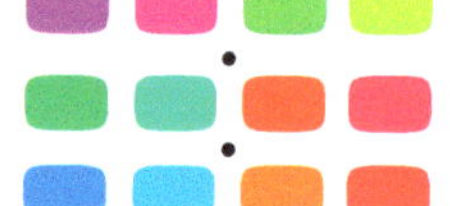

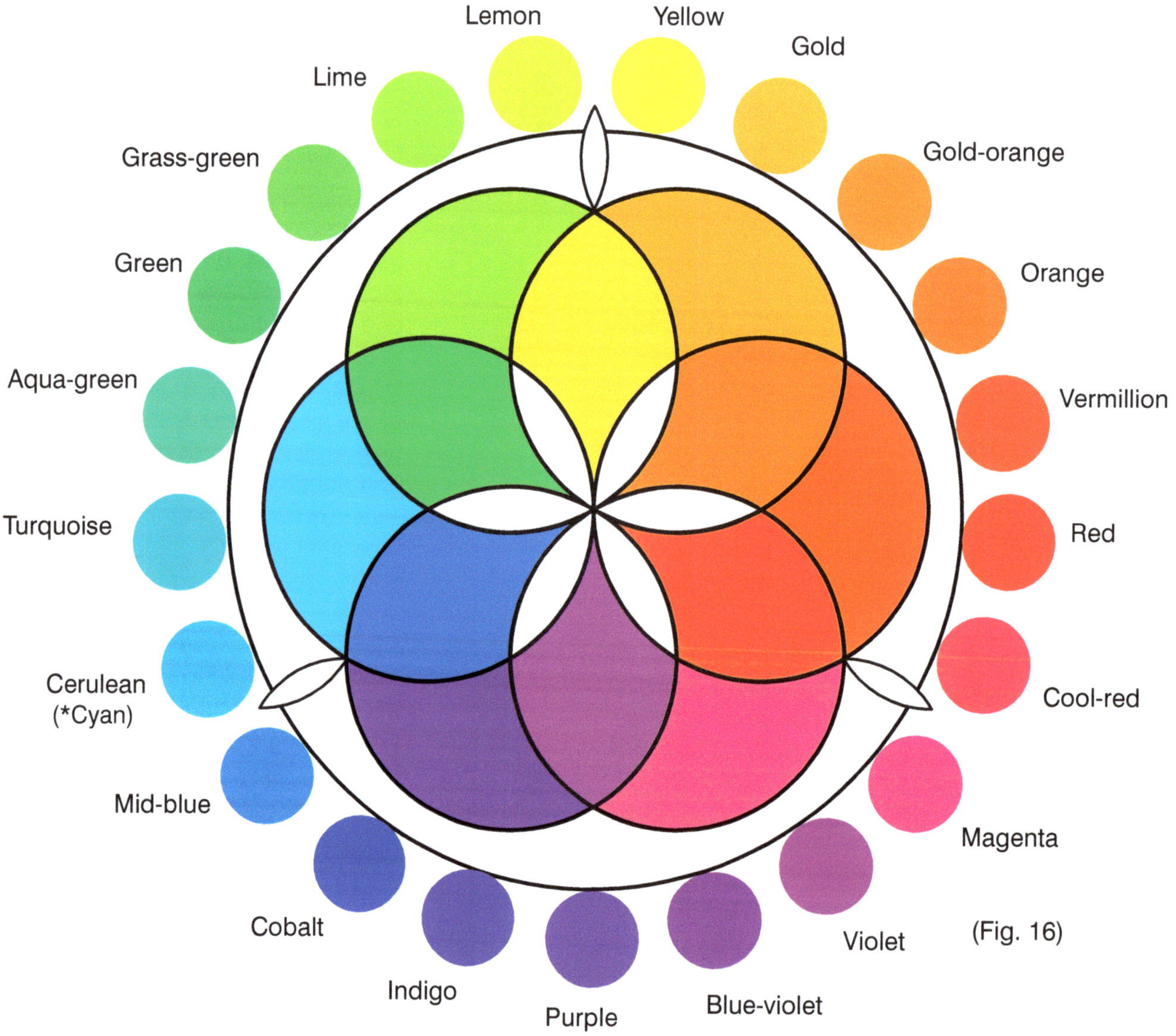

Lemon
Yellow
Gold
Gold-orange
Orange
Vermillion
Red
Cool-red
Magenta
Violet
Blue-violet
Purple
Indigo
Cobalt
Mid-blue
Cerulean (*Cyan)
Turquoise
Aqua-green
Green
Grass-green
Lime

(Fig. 16)

*(*Cyan is the ink hue close to Cerulean or Sky-blue)*

Utilising Colour Shades and Colour Tones.

Colour shading is one of the most rewarding and effective skills to master and apply in our artwork. Colours are effectively light frequencies and by learning how to apply variation in colour shading between specific hues, our artwork becomes far more dynamic and visually alive. There are no set rules to colour shading, so aim to experiment with complementary colours, as well as contrasting or supporting colours. Also, see the first seven masterclasses for a variety of examples and further shading techniques.

Colour shading also includes colour toning. For example, if we shade a medium or dark blue from heavy to light pigment, we get light blues in the tonal gradient. So shading may also be employed to produce a variation in tone, where a heavy pigmented or solid pencilling mixed with softer application results in a gradation to a lighter version of the same hue or colour, due to the underlying white paper. This effect is great for creating three-dimensional effects and for subtle shading on small objects to give a more dynamic nature or vibrancy to the artwork.

Colour tonations can be achieved either by shading mixed hues or tones, or by simply shading a colour inter-mixed or shaded with black on the dark end and leaving white paper on the lighter end. Also, dark blues and indigo blues can be shaded with lighter cyan or pastel blues for effects relative to these colours. Again, experiment with adjoining colours and hues, for example – red, orange and yellow. Another way to gain great effect is to pick a hue, miss one colour in the spectrum and then pick the next two like: magenta, (miss red) and then use orange and yellow.

Shading also emphasises the movement of energies or colour and caters to a more dynamic emotive effect, especially with vibrant hues, bright or warm colours.
Dark blue for example when shaded is more static in effect, with deep or dark blue shaded through to aqua or turquoise becoming more neutral or alive. If it was a warm indigo or ultramarine blue shaded with turquoise, then the combined shaded tonation would hold a slightly dynamic or vibrant effect overall, in terms of the resulting blended 'admixture'.

Dynamic and visually arresting effects can also be achieved by shading combinations of complementary colours in relation to the colour qualities detailed on the former pages and masterclasses. Shading effects utilising complementary opposites like blue and orange or yellow and violet can have a powerful balancing effect in mandalas and imagery, especially when matching image elements, totems, or overall subject matter. For example, violet and yellow used to colour imagery involving eagle or elk totems, or with expansive diagrams, crescent, teardrop, or dynamic elipse shapes would suit.

Another point to note is that in the very action of shading and toning we are working with emotional parts of ourself, in the process of what we are visually creating or bringing into being. So this is an important part of shading with colours and bringing some kind or creative uniqueness or colour signature to our art pieces. Always remember that colours are there to be freely experimented with, to have fun and allow our self-expressive capacity to become more multifaceted or mutlidimensional. A good deal of learnt skill to do with colour use and colour shading is often mastered by free association and practice, until we achieve the most pleasing or desireable effect.

Also, as colours are vibrational frequencies on a subtle level, colour shading is all about frequency attunement, augmentation or vibrational sensitivity. So colour shading and toning involves listening to our intuitive voicings and in effect, surrendering to colour contemplation and creative musing.

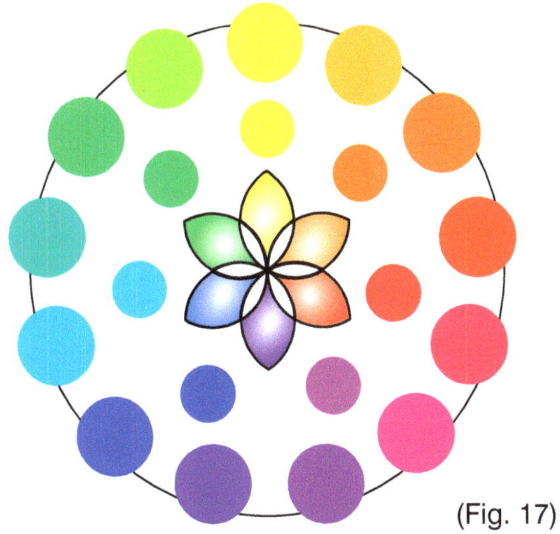

(Fig. 17)

Above we have a 13-point colour wheel for subtle frequency attunement. It is useful for abstract colour contemplation and to help unlock the more cryptic colour symbolism that lies beyond fixed or learnt structural models. It shares the interrelationship between 6 & 7 and graphically how we can have '2' closest neighbours as opposites for any one colour, instead of a fixed direct '1'. Moving beyond duality, this brings colouring in line with the '3' and includes the two magical numbers '7' and '13'.

www.ingramcontent.com/pod-product-compliance
Ingram Content Group UK Ltd.
Pitfield, Milton Keynes, MK11 3LW, UK
UKHW060025300726
14090UKWH00019B/1076